W9-DFU-648

Easy-to-Build
BIRDHOUSES

CHARLES SELF

DOVER PUBLICATIONS, INC.
Mineola, New York

ACKNOWLEDGMENTS

My thanks for help with various areas of this book go to Michael Burton, Jason Feldner, Tom Stauffer, Rob Lee, Jim Ray, George Gibson, and several others. Companies providing assistance included Hazelton Woodworks of Bruceton, Mills, WV, Thunderbird Wood (www.tbird-hardwoods.com), Freud, Bosch, Hitachi, Delta, DeWalt, Lee Valley (www.leevalley.com), McFeely's (www.mcfeelys.com), and Woodworker's Supply (www.woodworker.com).

Copyright

Copyright © 2007 by Charles Self
All rights reserved.

Bibliographical Note

Easy-to-Build Birdhouses is a new work, first published by Dover Publications, Inc., in 2007.

Library of Congress Cataloging-in-Publication Data

Self, Charles R.
    Easy-to-build birdhouses / Charles Self.
       p. cm.
     ISBN-13: 978-0-486-45182-4
     ISBN-10: 0-486-45182-8
      1. Birdhouses—Design and construction. I. Title.
  QL676.5.S367 2007
  690'.8927—dc22

2006046570

Manufactured in the United States of America
Dover Publications, Inc., 31 East 2nd Street, Mineola, N.Y. 11501

CONTENTS

INTRODUCTION

Most of the space in this book is taken up with plans and instructions for building the twelve included birdhouses. I've also included some detail on woods and other materials you'll need. Tool details are also relatively small in size, though I hope they're packed with information you need.

That said, let's go on to the subject matter: many birdhouse project books today seem to incorporate bright and shiny surfaces, either with glossy clear-spar-varnish-type finishes, or high-gloss enamel. These are great as yard and interior decorations, but my experience, and that of others, indicates that it is definitely not for the birds. The glistening surfaces startle them easily, so the fancier finished birdhouses are not as well received as those that aren't finished at all, or that are made of weathered wood.

Of the dozen birdhouses presented here, you'll find it's easy to add options: use them for decoration with clear finishes and nicer wood; use them for decoration with paint; use them for birds. My personal preference is for the latter, but rest assured that four or five years of nonattention will have most of those aimed for the first two categories working in the third category.

For the plans and their completion, construction is designed to use a minimum number of tools, while the finishes are varied to create different looks. The plans require mostly hand tools, and as few of those as is possible, though conversions to power tools are easily made, and some parts, such as turned spindles, may be replaced with shop-turned items. The essential factor overall is the lack of need for extensive shop equipment or woodworking experience. All are easily made by nonwoodworkers with only a few tools: a handsaw, a square, hammer, nails (or screwdriver and screws), a drill bit, and a drill or bit brace.

Birds nest at similar times around the world: early to mid-spring—give or take a few weeks—and the weather in your area helps determine the qualities your birdhouses need. Traditional types of birdhouses are easily made, though, and work decently almost throughout the world. For later-nesting birds, some sun protection is essential, while some heat retention is good for those birds that nest earlier. The same material does the insulation job in both cases: wood. Simply put, if you are going to produce a birdhouse that has a metal roof, put that metal over at least a ¼"-thick piece of wood.

The specifications go on from there. Although you may want to build for décor, I'm going to show you how to build for the birds. The two can work together nicely, or you can leave out the features you feel are really "for the birds" if you're building indoor decorations.

Enjoy.

CHARLIE SELF
2006

CHAPTER ONE
WHAT THE BIRDS LIKE

We begin this series of projects by looking at what a birdhouse needs most, from a bird's point of view. In general, my aim in this book is to ensure that the birds are happy with your efforts.

Snugness. This one is simple enough. A snug birdhouse has just enough room for the nesting materials, the bird, and the young birds, and not much extra space, but is not so cramped that there's no room for several babies and the parent. Birds have size needs (just as we do), and they react, live, and reproduce better when those size needs are met. You'll find size requirements for most types of desirable nesting birds in this book, and changing a few sizes, sometimes only one, can make a single birdhouse design suitable for a number of birds.

General comfort. Protection from wind, rain, and snow—as well as sleet and hail—is a desirable feature, with the opening oriented to the direction preferred by the species of bird. Ventilation is an important factor here. Ventilation slots or holes cut well up in the birdhouse help to maintain air movement with the front opening and with floor drain openings.

Slow reaction to temperature changes. Probably better than slow is "slower" reaction to temperature swings. This means you don't want a roofing material that heats up so fast it cooks the birds or makes them ill from the heat. The same with cold. Birds can stand a reasonable amount of cool, but we don't want them turning gelid on the nest. Use housing materials that retard heat movement in either direction. That doesn't necessarily mean you need to build and insulate a huge birdhouse, but using natural materials such as solid wood is a start. Proper location, out of direct sun and wind, is another salient point.

Dryness. Easy enough. For those birds that insist on enclosed nesting spaces, try to provide corner or other draining in the bottom of the birdhouse for any incidental water entry, and orient the house so openings are not in direct line with driven rain or snow or ice.

Protection from predators. I don't suggest you shoot your neighbor's cats, but you want to make it more difficult for cats and snakes to gain entry or even access to the birdhouse. Leave off the exterior perches, for a start. Mount the house on a slick pole, as far up as the desired species will accept. Use predator guards—a cone of light metal wrapped around the pole, wide side down—where possible. These keep snakes from slithering up the pole.

Suitable distance from the ground to emulate natural nesting spaces. Some birds like 3, 4, 5 or 6 feet while others prefer 20. There is seldom much nest interchange (of course, most of the birds that nest low are smaller, while those that nest high tend to be larger—like all generalities, that one has major holes, I know).

Ease of entry. The house needs to be easy for the bird to get into and out of, while also being difficult for snakes to enter. It's always nice when you can confine entry to one or two bird species. This sometimes works, but it often doesn't. Keep the entry holes as small as possible for the species desired, and rough up the exterior around the hole so the bird's claws have something to grip. You might place a small perch inside the entry hole, too.

Appearance. Birds are a bit like auto and truck drivers. Don't startle them and they're a lot happier. Give them something too shiny, and they tend to flutter off. They may or may not return. Make them a birdhouse that fits into the natural scheme of things, and they're more likely to check it out and stay. Anyone who has ever seen bluebirds house-hunting knows that this works. I've seen bluebird pairs build in two newer houses, only to go down the fence line to the most dilapidated—to human eyes—derelict chunk of redwood boards around, and set up housekeeping in the near wreck more times than I want to count.

Getting the size right is of importance if you're aiming to attract birds, though most birds are willing to adapt to slightly unsuitably sized nesting areas. The chart on the next page gives some sizes for birds that we generally welcome in yards and around houses.

A cautionary tale: there are many more welcome birds, and there are some cautions about the birds listed in the chart, especially the larger woodpeckers, such as the flicker and the red-headed. Both of these birds, once established, can be amazingly destructive of property and very difficult to discourage. On a personal note, I've had lots of damage to my woodworking shop created by flickers enlarging openings in the eaves, and on the soffit and fascia, in order to get into the attic area of the shop for nesting purposes. I have yet to find an effective way to seal the area and evict the birds, and the larger holes have brought a plague of squirrels with them. They also damaged one corner of that house badly, forcing replacement of some siding and a couple of corner boards.

There are many more birds that you will find flitting around a yard, including doves and wrens, some sparrows, chickadees, nuthatches, phoebes, bluebirds, swallows, and many of the woodpeckers, including the downy and the hairy. Not all are birds that nest in houses. Some birds are desirable, while others are less so. Starlings are a plague on many feeders and around yards, where they adapt quickly to conditions favorable to almost any small birds, too often ousting the more favored birds.

Birdhouses provide spring care for birds and a nesting site that helps them keep their numbers up.

When you say "C'mon to my house" to birds, you're making a commitment that helps keep a continuing natural balance on things; gives you enjoyment in constructing wood projects; gives you an excuse to collect tools that are handy for other projects, non-bird related; and also gives you a shot at great enjoyment in watching their numbers increase. It's hard to describe the enjoyment you'll get when you note a declining species (which bluebirds were, some twenty years ago), having several batches of chicks each year, teaching them to fly, feed on their own, and generally introducing them to bird life. But it is better than just good.

Birdhouse Sizing

Species	House floor (inches)	House depth (inches)	Hole above Floor	Diameter of Hole	Height above Ground (feet)
American Kestrel	8x8	15	12–13	3	10–20
Bluebird	5x5	8	6	1½	5–10
Chickadee	4x4	8–10	6–8	1⅛	6–15
Titmouse	4x4	8–10	6–8	1¼	6–15
Nuthatch	4x4	8–10	6–8	1¼	12–20
Bewick's Wren	4x4	6–8	4–6	1–1¼	6–10
Carolina Wren	4x4	6–8	4–6	1½	6–10
Purple Martin	6x6	6	2	2½	10–15
Crested Flycatcher	6x6	8–10	6–8	2	8–20
Flicker	7x7	16–18	14–16	2½	6–20
Red-Headed Woodpecker	6x6	12–15	9–12	2	12–20
Downy Woodpecker	4x4	9–12	6–8	1¼	6–20
Robin	6x8	8	(1+ sides open)	NA	6–15
Barn Swallow	6x6	6	(1+ sides open)	NA	8–12
Phoebe	6x6	6	(1+ sides open)	NA	8–12
Screech Owl	8x8	12–15	9–12	3	10–30
Wood Duck	10–18	10–24	12–16	4	10–20

Chapter Two
Materials: Wood Isn't All of It

There are a limited number of truly useful birdhouse woods, though you can actually use almost any wood, including a multitude of exotics that has a reasonable chance of surviving more than two seasons out-of-doors. But the expectation that a birdhouse should last only a couple to three years is not a good one, as it may take that long to attract birds to the nesting area. Some woods do well when painted, others do well when left alone. Of the dozen or so suitable woods, pine is probably the cheapest in most areas, but woods such as walnut and white oak give some unusual talking points, as do woods such as mahogany. On a personal basis, I prefer easily worked woods for birdhouses, which tends to mean using sharp tools and softwood, either a pine, cedar, or cypress. Some are better than others at what we need. Pines do not last for an exceptionally long time, though I've got one pine birdhouse up in Virginia (south central region) that has been in place for over five years. It is unfinished and doing fine. There are also some redwood bluebird houses there that are outlasting the locust fence posts they were originally hung on, nearly sixteen years ago.

I've worked to keep open end grain from standing vertically in my plans (sometimes, as with backs, it is unavoidable), which helps keep water from penetrating and starting a destructive freeze thaw cycle in winter. That helps any wood, regardless of its durability. Otherwise, durable woods such as some cedars, cypress, redwood, walnut, white oak, and others last the longest.

I'm not providing furniture-makers' detail on woods here, as that is unnecessary, as is providing information on nondurable hardwoods. Photographs of some of the woods described in this chapter have been reproduced in full color on the inside front cover.

CEDARS

Alaska cedar is the starting point for this group of durable softwoods. Growing from the Pacific Coast region of North America from southeastern Alaska down to southern Oregon, *Chamaecyparis nootkatensis* is straight-grained and fine-textured. The sapwood is white shading to yellow, with a bright yellow heart-wood. Often called yellow cedar, it is taken from a tree about 80' to 100' in height. There is little difference in appearance of heartwood and sapwood. Alaska cedar is moderately heavy, very resistant to decay, and is moderately hard. After seasoning, during which it shrinks very little, Alaska cedar is quite stable. It is not an aromatic cedar (its odor is mildly unpleasant, but after cutting, it fades to a potato-like smell). It works easily with both hand and power tools. For birdhouses, Alaska cedar is an excellent choice.

Incense cedar, *Libocedrus decurrens*, is from a tree 80' to 150' in height, and 3' or more in diameter. The sapwood is white to a cream and the heartwood is a light brown, often tingeing toward red for a pink overall hue. The wood has a fine, uniform texture, and a spicy aroma when it is cut or sanded. Unlike Alaska cedar, and more like the remainder of American cedars, incense cedar is light in weight, fairly low in strength, with low shock resistance and not a whole lot of stiffness (for a wood: don't whack yourself on the head to test hardness or see if the board flexes). Shrinkage is modest, and there is little checking and warping during seasoning. Incense cedar is locally low in cost, *if* you can accept its peckiness (localized pockets of decay that do not spread after the wood is dried). The wood works easily with conventional (tool steel) tools and with carbide tools. It makes superb small box material, including boxes that become birdhouses.

Port Orford cedar, *Chamaecyparis lawsoniana,* has heartwood that is light yellow shading to a pale brown. Sapwood is thin and hard to discern from the heartwood. The wood is non-resinous from a tree up to 160' in height and 5' in diameter. The wood is fine-textured, with generally straight grain, and has a pleasant and spicy odor. Port Orford cedar is superbly resistant to decay, moderately light in weight, and is stiff, moderately strong, and hard. The wood works easily with conventional hand and power tools. It is excellent for birdhouses.

Red cedar, Eastern, is aromatic cedar, and grows everywhere in the East except Maine and Florida. *Juniperus virginiana* is the major species of Eastern red cedar, but in some South Atlantic and Gulf Coastal Plains areas, you will also find *Juniperus silicicola*. Both are sold as red cedar without further identification. The tree is small, usually not more than 40 feet tall. The heartwood of the red cedar is bright red, sometimes almost purple, tending to a duller red. The thin sapwood is almost white, and clearly defined. The wood is moderately heavy, moderately low in strength, and is hard. It seasons well, has high shock resistance, and low stiffness, and a tight, fine texture. The grain is said to be straight, but after cutting hundreds of red cedars, I've yet to see any run straight for much longer than a couple feet. The wood is easily worked with conventional tools of all kinds, but will deposit lots of pitch if not seasoned well. Regardless, it lists as a non-resinous wood among botanical classifiers. The many, many knots deflect the grain. Red cedar is an excellent birdhouse wood.

Red cedar, Western, *Thuja plicata,* is also called canoe cedar, giant arbor vitae, or shinglewood. The tree may be 160' (and more) tall and 4' thick. The aroma is pungent and attractive. Heartwood is reddish brown to dull brown; sapwood is nearly white, and narrow. The wood is straight, but has a coarse, uniform texture. Shrinkage is slight, and the resulting wood is light in weight, moderately soft, low in strength. Heartwood is exceptionally resistant to decay. Western red cedar works easily—most red cedar shakes are hand-split—with all conventional tools, both hand and power. It is excellent for birdhouses.

White cedar, Northern and Atlantic, are usually clumped together at sales time. Northern white cedar is *Thuja occidentalis* (also called, simply, cedar, and arbor vitae). Southern white cedar is *Chamaecyparis thyiodes* (also Southern white cedar, swamp cedar, and boat cedar). The trees are about 65' tall, and not over 24" in diameter. White cedar heartwood is light brown, and the sapwood is nearly white, and forms only a thin band. The wood is lightweight, soft, and not strong. Shock resistance is low, but shrinkage during seasoning is low, and the wood is stable afterwards. This cedar takes paint well—most others require a coat of shellac to prevent bleed-through of resins—and like the rest of the cedars, works easily with conventional tools, both hand and power. Heartwood is exceptionally durable, so the wood is superb for birdhouses.

Cypress is also called baldcypress, Southern cypress, red cypress, yellow cypress, and white cypress. It is a deciduous—leaf-dropping—softwood, of medium size rarely reaching 145' in height, and more often 65' to 130'. It has a buttressed trunk—cypress knees are famous—that may be as much as 5' in diameter. The wood is moderate in cost within much of its range. Current early-growth heartwood cypress is not as durable as old-growth, but still lasts extremely well. I built some cypress birdhouses recently, and expect them

to endure for many years. Cypress is another tree with only a small sapwood band, which is nearly white, contrasting strongly with the light yellowish brown to dark reddish brown, brown, or even chocolate of the heartwood. *Taxodium distichum* is moderately heavy, moderately strong, and moderately hard. It's easy to work with conventional hand and power tools, and shrinks a bit more than cedars, but still within a very small range. Durability (decay resistance) ranges from truly great for old-growth cypress to moderately good for new-growth materials. Cypress is great for boxes of most sizes: of course, boxes include birdhouses and nesting shelves. It is not always easy to find, and I've never seen it in any of the big box stores for home builders. You need to locate a wood dealer—oddly enough, this softwood is often sold by hardwood dealers.

PINES

Pines are woods most of us know, both as woodworkers, and as people living in homes with wood products. Pines are more prolific now than any other wood and are probably used for more things than most other woods. Some pine species are very soft and low in strength, though still strong enough for building construction. They accept shaping amazingly well, so a great many items from birdhouses to doors are produced from pine today. In addition, pines come in species that are almost as hard as a mid-range hardwood (many of the yellow pines) that do not take nails easily, and that are not as easy to shape, but that are wonderfully strong and useful in many ways, again, including birdhouse construction.

Pine, Eastern White, *Pinus strobes*, is also known as white pine, Northern white pine, Weymouth pine, and soft pine. The tree may be 100' in height, and 30" through the trunk. Heartwood is light brown, often tinged red, and turns considerably darker when exposed to light and air. The wood has reasonably uniform texture and is straight-grained. It kiln dries easily, with little shrinkage, and ranks quite high in stability. It is also easy to work with all sharp tools, and is easily glued with almost all woodworking adhesives. Eastern white pine is lightweight, moderately soft, moderately low in strength, and has a low resistance to shock. The hobby woodworker finds that it works easily with conventional tools, but resin tends to build, even from thoroughly dried white pine. It takes finish well, especially if you seal—with shellac—all the knots. Cleaning blades and bits frequently helps prevent burning. When aged, Eastern white pine is a pumpkin color, and often derives a name—pumpkin pine—from that color. White pine is one of the moderate-cost woods and comes in many grades. On top of all that, it's the fastest growing tree in its range, often spurting up a foot and a half a year.

Pine, Pitch, *Pinus rigida*, is the pine most closely associated with hollers and hardscrabble. It is a resinous wood with a brownish red heartwood. The sapwood is thick and a light yellow, while the wood of the pitch pine is moderately heavy fringing toward heavy, moderately strong, stiff, and hard, with moderately high shock resistance. Shrinkage is moderate and it is good for birdhouses; expect it to last several years without finishing. The wood works easily with conventional hand and power tools, but the build-up of resin is quick and must be cleared from blades frequently.

Pine, Ponderosa, *Pinus ponderosa*, is another large tree, often reaching 230' in height, with a trunk about 30 inches in diameter. This is a yellow pine, similar to white pines in appearance and properties. The heartwood is a light, reddish brown, and the wide sapwood band is nearly white, varying to pale yellow. It is usually straight-grained, and has modest shrinkage during drying. The wood is uniform in texture, with little tendency to warp or twist. It works very nicely with conventional hand and power tools and resin build-up is within reason (it always pays to keep clearing resin when working with pines, cedars, and other sometimes non-resinous woods that have sticky sap). Although it is used mainly for lumber, this clear wood makes good birdhouses. Ponderosa pine should be painted or varnished for birdhouse use.

Pine, Southern, is actually a group of species that have similar characteristics and grow in many of the same areas. Trees range up to 90 and even 100' in height, and trunks are as much as 36" in diameter. Southern pines are moderately durable in the weather, so are great for birdhouse use. All also tend to build up resin on tools.

Longleaf pine, or *Pinus palustris*, shortleaf pine, or *P. echinata*, loblolly pine, or *P. taeda*, slash pine, or *P. elliotti*, all fit in the industry grading standards class the lumber of those species, and some other very minor species, as Southern pine. The wood is reddish brown heartwood, and a yellow-white sapwood. Southern pines are heavy, strong, stiff, and hard. All are stable when properly dried. The Southern Forest Products Association has strict grading standards, including wood density ratings. The wood is harder to work with than other pines, and resists nail penetration like locust, but otherwise is easy to work with conventional hand and power tools. Pitch build-up is moderate. An excellent birdhouse wood category.

Pine, Western White, *Pinus monticola*, may reach 125' in height, with a 3' diameter trunk. The heartwood is a cream color to light reddish brown, and darkens on exposure to light and air. The sapwood is yellow-white. The wood is straight-grained, easy to work, easily kiln dried, and stable after drying. Western white pine is moderately low in strength, moderately soft, moderately stiff, and lightweight. It glues easily and finishes well. Shrinkage is moderately large, but the wood is stable after drying. Overall, this is a marvelous wood for bird-

houses and many other woodworking projects. Western white pine is also relatively low in cost, and requires only conventional tools, but needs paint or other finish for exterior use.

REDWOOD

Redwood is pretty much tied with cypress and the cedars as the ideal birdhouse wood. Its cost keeps it from winning, though.

Redwood is an immense tree. Tree size is often 300 feet, with trunks nearly ten feet in diameter. *Sequoia sempervirens* has a closely related species, giant sequoia (*Sequoiadendron giganteum*), that grows in a very limited area. The heartwood of redwood varies from a light cherry red to a dark mahogany color; the narrow sapwood is almost white. Old-growth redwood is moderately light in weight, moderately strong and stiff, and moderately hard. The wood is easy to work, and is generally very straight-grained, and shrinks and swells very little. Heartwood from old-growth trees has extremely high decay resistance, but heartwood from second-growth trees ranges from resistant to moderately resistant. Most redwood lumber is used for building, and it is made into siding, sash, doors, finish, and containers. Redwood is absolutely great for many smaller outdoor woodworking projects, including birdhouses and feeders. Redwood works easily with conventional power or hand tools, and resin build-up is slight, but present. The wood splits, but doesn't splinter easily, so you can often work with less damage to your hands. When you do get a splinter, though, the resin needs to be cleared quickly from the wound—I use a peroxide boil: simply keep pouring peroxide on it until it quits foaming, wait 30 minutes, and do it again.

SPRUCE

Spruce, Eastern, includes red (*Picea rubens*), white (*P. glauca*), and black (*P. mariana*) spruces, sold as a single species. The wood dries easily, and is stable after drying, with moderately lightweight, easy-working characteristics, moderate shrinkage, and moderate strength. It is light in color, with little difference visible between the heartwood and sapwood. The largest use for Eastern spruce is pulpwood, but some does find its way into building construction, general millwork, boxes, crates, and even piano sounding boards. For birdhouse use, it rates high, but needs protection for long-term use (more than five years).

Spruce, Sitka, is a large tree up to 290' tall, and sometimes 16' in diameter. *Picea sitchensis* heartwood is a light, pinkish brown; sapwood is creamy white, and shades gradually into the heartwood. The sapwood may be 6" wide. The wood has a fine, uniform texture, and is generally straight-grained, with no distinct taste or odor. It is moderately light in weight, moderately low in bending and compressive strength, moderately stiff.

Shrinkage is small, and straight, clear-grained pieces are easily obtained. It works very nicely indeed with sharp conventional hand and power tools, and makes superb boxes of almost any size, which, as always, covers birdhouses. The lack of taste and odor makes it excellent for canisters and similar projects. It glues up nicely, takes stain well, and finishes with both paint and varnishes. Sitka spruce is on the costly side for softwoods.

DURABLE DOMESTIC HARDWOODS

Locust, Black, is a wood that is often overlooked for birdhouse purposes and relegated to fence posts. *Robinia pseudoacacia* is small, with a ropy looking bark, seldom exceeding 55' tall. Girths may reach 42", but usually are no more than 2'. Locust sapwood is narrow and creamy in color, and fresh-cut heartwood ranges from greenish yellow to dark brown. The wood darkens to a good-looking medium gold-brown. The wood is coarse-textured, and straight-grained, and weighs about the same as oak. Black locust is a very hard, very heavy wood, with very high overall strength and stiffness. Heartwood has a high decay resistance. It is fairly hard to machine, and much easier to work with carbide tipped power tools. Shrinkage and swelling are both moderate; it glues well and holds nails and screws snugly. Locust also bends well, and takes a decent finish without excess work. Today, most locust is destined for use as fence posts, rails, crossties, and fuel. Its classic durability makes it an ideal wood for birdhouses.

Oaks, white oak group, includes white oak (*Quercus alba*); chestnut oak (*Q. prinus*); post oak (*Q. stellata*); overcup oak (*Q. lyrata*); swamp chestnut oak (*Q. michauxii*); bur oak; (*Q. macrocarpa*); chinkapin oak (*Q. muehlenbergii*); swamp white oak (*Q. bicolor*); and live oak (*Q. virginiana*). *Q. alba* may stand as much as 115' tall, but almost never goes higher. Trunks may be 5' in diameter. Heartwood is grayish brown, and the sapwood, which may be two or more inches thick, is nearly white. Tyloses plug the wood so no water, or other liquids, can flow through the heartwood. White oak is a hard, tough, straight-grained wood. It takes screws and nails well, if pilot holes are drilled, and generally looks great. White oak is durable, takes a good finish, with no filler required. It glues easily with all woodworking adhesives, *except* epoxy. The presence of tannin—tannic acid—means you need to use stainless steel screws and nails, or aluminum or brass, in outdoor projects, to prevent the metals from turning black. Never use soap to lubricate a screw or nail in white oak: the soap draws water, and increases chances of problems. Green white oak bends easily, and rip sawing is a simple matter with a sharp blade and a slow feed. Always make certain your blades are sharp, and correctly sharpened so they'll hold their edges. Use carbide edged tools, whenever you can.

Sassafras is probably better known for its qualities as a beverage ingredient than as a durable wood; *Sassafras albidum* resembles black ash in color, grain, and texture. Trees range from small to moderately large depending on growing conditions, with a medium, and usual, tree reaching no more than 50' high, with a 40"-diameter trunk. Sassafras works easily with hand tools, but planing has a tendency to lift the grain if tool edges aren't kept very sharp. It glues well, sands easily, and takes a fine finish. Drill pilot holes for screws and nails. Sassafras sapwood is light yellow, while heartwood ranges from dull gray to brown and dark brown, occasionally with a red tinge. The wood is moderately light for a hardwood, weak in bending and endwise compression, soft, brittle, and durable. It is not useful where weight must be borne, but is a good turning wood, with unusual grain patterns. It is thus twice useful for birdhouses, as some people like to turn their birdhouses. The small amount of oils in the wood gives it a characteristic odor: to check what you're getting, run a scraper over the wood. It is aromatic, with a medicinal odor that is mild enough to be quite pleasant.

Walnut, Black is North America's premier furniture wood, and usually its most costly. Walnut trees, under ideal conditions, can reach 150 feet with a six-foot diameter, but it's more usual to find them touching 100' with a 3' diameter. *Juglans nigra* has a nearly white sapwood up to 3" thick in open grown trees. The heartwood varies, from purplish brown with thin, darker veins, to a grayish brown, and an orange-brown. The grain is fairly open and straight, usually without figure. Walnut is heavy, hard and stiff, straight-grained and easily worked with almost all tools, power or hand, and is stable once seasoned. Shock resistance is excellent, which is why many generations of rifle and shotgun users have used walnut stocks. Black walnut dust can be rough on the eyes, so wear goggles during use, as well as a dust mask. Take shallow cuts and multiple passes when jointing or routing to avoid tearout. Use a backerboard on the miter fence when crosscutting to reduce chipping. Keep glue squeeze-out to a minimum. It is surprisingly durable.

EXOTICS FOR BIRDHOUSES

Jarrah is an Australian offering to the world. *Eucalyptus marginata* has a small range, along the coast south of Perth, in Australia, but it is very common there. The tree is a modest size for a eucalyptus, seldom going over 150' (other eucalyptus species may reach 200'). The heartwood is medium to dark brown after age and exposure take over, but freshly cut, it's a uniform pink to dark red, a rich mahogany color. Sapwood is pale in color and very narrow in older trees, wider in newer growth. Grain is often interlocked and wavy, and texture is even, but moderately coarse. The wood glues satisfactorily, but drill pilot holes if nailing or driving screws—it tends to splinter in some situations. Gum veins create some problems in this hard, heavy wood that rates as very resistant to termite attack. The wood is difficult to work by hand because of the high density and interlocking grain. Jarrah is often used for heavy construction, exterior and interior millwork, furniture, turnery, and decorative veneers. It might well make excellent turned or board birdhouses.

Mahogany, African, is *Khaya ivorensis, K. anthotheca* and the heartwood is pale pink to a dark red-brown. Grain is often interlocked, and the texture is medium coarse, comparable to that of American mahogany. The wood seasons easily, but machining properties may vary. Nailing and gluing properties are good, and it's moderately durable. Most uses are for furniture, boat work, cabinetry, interior finish, and veneer. A definite must try for a birdhouse.

Teak, *Tectona grandis*, is now heavily grown in plantations. It is a tree of variable size, and may reach 125' when well grown, with a trunk as much as 6' in diameter. Wood texture is coarse and uneven, and teak has an oily feel. Grain may be straight or wavy. Burma teak tends to be uniform golden brown, while teak from other areas is a darker brown, with more black markings. Teak is strong, works well, but the silica in the wood dulls tools quickly, so carbide edges are helpful. The wood holds nails and screws well, but pilot holes are needed for ease of working. Teak is a costly wood currently used in the construction of expensive boats, lawn furniture, flooring, and decorative objects, and will be reasonable in cost for birdhouses only because of the small amounts needed.

Using the correct adhesive means a long-lasting birdhouse. Epoxy is only used in small quantities in unusual situations. Epoxy holds the fence posts up in the flycatcher house.

Fasteners

Wood glues hold wood joints together, so adhesives are essential to some birdhouse construction (there are mechanical fasteners, and there are joints that do not always require glue—some forms of dovetailing, usually—but for most purposes, our joints are made with one of the wood glues, including epoxy, though mostly with glues such as Titebond II, Titebond III, and the polyurethanes).

Wood Selection for Gluing

Producing birdhouse projects successfully, whether a single project or a dozen different projects (or one project a dozen different times) means an appropriate adhesive, correct clamping, and plenty of drying time. Woods to be joined must match well: too much difference in moisture content of wood creates problems, as do too great differences in wood structure. For example, teak, with high silicone and oil contents, does not bond well with any other woods. It is even difficult to bond to itself, and is usually best served with one of the top grade epoxies.

When the same species of wood is used, you get the best gluing results, the longest and strongest hold. All boards may be pine or fir or oak or walnut. If part is walnut and part is pine, difficulties may arise, though with small cross sections, as in most birdhouses, difficulties aren't going to be overwhelming if all wood is dried to about the same moisture content.

None of our projects have extensive wood movement problems because even the larger birdhouses are small as wood projects go. The basic need for wood glues when building birdhouses are good strength and high water resistance or even waterproofing. We'll look at those glues only.

Selecting a Woodworking Glue

Inexpensive, water-resistant glues such as Titebond II, from Franklin International, are superb for the birdhouse builder. Titebond III is waterproof and might be even better, though it does cost a little bit more.

Titebond II wood glue is a heat-resistant, waterproof liquid polyaliphatic resin glue that is sufficiently waterproof to be used everywhere but below water lines. It is similar in joint appearance to other yellow glues, but sets even more rapidly. The chemists have provided Titebond II Extend for those of us who don't move very quickly during assembly. Initial tack is strong, set is fast (about five minutes), and these chemically cross-linked glues do not gum badly during sanding. Clamp for about one half hour. They are a bit more temperature critical, at least on the cold side, than are regular aliphatic resin glues: I used Titebond II for some winter projects and got chalky-appearing excess glue when shop temperatures were below about 60 degrees F.

Titebond II is a strong, water-resistant glue.

Titebond II and Titebond III are modestly more expensive than standard Titebond. Such waterproof and highly water-resistant glues are not really for everyday use, though a lot of woodworkers assume that total water resistance is better than moderately high water resistance. If you ever need to disassemble any project, for any reason, you cannot do so by using water as a solvent on the glue. Once dried, Titebond II is pretty much water-as-solvent proof, as are Titebond III, the foaming polyurethane glues, epoxy, resorcinol, and plastic resin.

Polyurethane Glues

I've tried most of the polyurethane glues and tend not to agree with those who find them ideal for everything, though they're excellent for many birdhouse uses. They're a shade more difficult to use than yellow glues, in part because of foaming and in part because water clean-up doesn't work, and they're much more costly. There is also the possible need for misting of surfaces when wood is extremely dry. While less is needed, there is usually no need for the kind of waterproofing they do. If you decide to make projects in this book and want to make them suitable for use below the waterline, then you want to use polyurethane, but otherwise, our birdhouses simply do not need the degree of waterproofing these glues give. For the most part, epoxy is also not needed, but it does have other helpful qualities, including gap filling, which polyurethane types do not offer.

Epoxy Adhesives

Epoxies aren't particularly handy for most of our birdhouse making projects, but new formulas have been developed that aid in using these adhesives, and in those areas where the glue itself can be used as a support for a project part, epoxy truly stands out. I find epoxies excellent gap fillers, and wonderful for attaching metal parts to wood. Epoxies are two-part adhesives, a liquid hardener that is added to a liquid resin. Cure is by chemical reaction. Heat is produced during the reaction.

Mix only as much as you will use immediately. Epoxies are costly.

If you decide to use a wood such as teak, epoxies simplify matters. Epoxies are made to fit about any bonding need, in moderate temperature applications.

Set time is important in wood adhesives. One of the reasons epoxies missed early popularity was that most are fast-set types, setting in under five minutes. Such speed is fine for many things, including very small woodworking projects and repairs, but is a mess maker on larger projects. Cost, toxicity, and mess are the main limiting factors in epoxy use.

Epoxies are very toxic, limiting uses in some shops, including mine. They are also messy, a problem easily solved. Wear thin plastic gloves (go with nitrile: they avoid chances of latex allergies showing up, are much stronger—sometimes reusable and are not harmed by most solvents [as some latex gloves are]). They are available in packs of 100, to avoid the hand mess. Clean up quickly with acetone (if you can't find acetone elsewhere, get nail polish remover) for other messiness, keeping the gloves on. Make sure all mixing containers and sticks are disposable.

Working with dense woods or with exotics such as teak, you don't have a real choice. Epoxy is it, unless you use polyurethane. Clamping pressure is light, working time is adjustable to as much as ninety minutes, gap filling is superb, strength is incredible, and the resulting glue line is either clear or an amber color.

In summary: epoxy doesn't shrink, so it is a good gap filler. Some is formed as putty, filling the largest gaps, though tight joint fits are still better for long project life. Although epoxy has a clear joint line, good heat resistance, and remains impervious to water and most chemicals, it is also expensive, hard to use, and may present fume problems if used in large amounts.

Using Glues

The selection of the correct glue is important, but so are the application of the glue and the clamping of the parts. Also important is working with a tight-fitting joint so there are no gap filling problems or joints weakened by thick expanses of nothing but glue. We want our birdhouse projects to last.

Make any glue selection on the qualities your project needs most.

For general uses, liquid yellow glues and polyvinyl acetate (white resin) glues are best.

For greatest waterproofing, choose epoxy or polyurethane—polyurethane first unless the epoxies fill some other specific need such as great unsupported strength or gap filling. Epoxies are too costly for general use.

The type of glue chosen determines method of application, though most may be applied with a brush, stick, or roller. Joint surfaces first must be checked. If the joint surface is a tight fit, clean off all dust, oil, old glue, loosened and torn grain, and chips. Any cutting that has to be done is done as close as possible to the time of gluing and assembly.

A test assembly is a good idea—once glue is added, correcting mistakes is messy. If mistakes creep in and glue sets, mistakes must stay.

Before you apply the glue, test assemble to see whether the unit can be assembled within the time required for the chosen adhesive. If a glue has a ten-minute open time, assembly must be completed within that time limit. The thicker the glue you spread, generally, the longer the open assembly time. If wood is very porous or dry, open assembly time decreases.

If the test assembly takes more than the allotted time, change the method of gluing or the type of adhesive used so there's enough time to complete and clamp the assembly.

Mix, where required, all adhesives according to the maker's directions, and as accurately as possible. Spread evenly over the surfaces to be joined.

On a personal recommendation basis, I'd say go with Titebond II for all birdhouse construction that needs glue. It is powerfully water-resistant and grips extremely well.

Clamps

The following section rightly belongs under tools, but is placed here because the major use of clamps in woodworking is to hold parts together while glues bond. There are other uses, but this is the primary one.

Many styles of woodworking clamps are available, and many have changed in recent decades. Many haven't changed in decades, though. Woodworking clamps fall into one of these categories: bar clamps, hand screws, C clamps, and band clamps.

You'll find plenty of variations on each theme, with pipe clamps, picture frame clamps, miter clamps, and a slew of others. The largest number of variations probably fall in the bar clamp range, though recently, miter and frame clamps seem to be gaining. Both the Adjustable Clamp Company and American Clamping Corporation catalogs show many variants of most clamps, with a wide range of sizes and accessory assemblies.

Clamps are something one collects over the years, buying and begging as they're needed for projects. If you're buying clamps that aren't needed immediately, figure out how the new tools will be used, where, and how often. Once that's determined, selection of clamp type just about falls in your lap, becoming nearly (but not quite) automatic. We're going to jump right on past those clamps that are not at all useful in birdhouse making.

Cam Clamps

Cam clamps are quick-action light duty, light pressure bar clamps that are close to ideal to the kind of light

This is just a corner of the wide world of clamps.

C clamp.

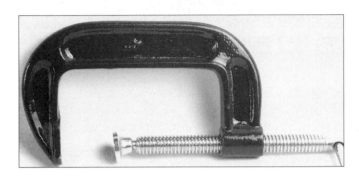

One-hand clamps are exceptionally useful when building birdhouses.

A band clamp is used for jobs like gluing up the decagonal birdhouse.

Materials: Wood Isn't All of It 17

Spring clamps do an admirable job of clamping backerboards tightly to a piece being drilled. This prevents splintering at the rear of the hole.

Small bar clamps are always handy to have around with box-type projects like birdhouses.

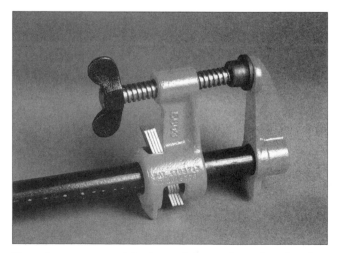

Pipe clamps are good for larger jobs, and cost less than bar clamps.

work carried out in instrument making. I've seen guitar makers use these in profusion, and for light box making (as in birdhouses) there is little else that is as easy to use. The lever that activates the cam provides only light pressure, but, then, most of these clamps have a bar no longer than 12", though I have seen a few around 16" or so. They are actually available in sizes up to and past 30", and some come with deep throats for larger work, and many have cork or other soft facing materials on the pressure faces.

C Clamps

For years, I felt the best uses for C clamps were in welding. Some are, I imagine, but there is also a number of woodworking clamping jobs they do well. For the most part, C clamps need some kind of protection between the work and the clamping surface, and also to help spread the pressure, as C clamps do provide a very strong pressure in a very confined area. C clamps are low cost, thus useful where lots of relatively small clamps are needed.

Hand Screws

Hand screws are one of the most versatile, and one of the most underused, woodworker's clamps. The wood jaws and steel threads allow different angles to be readily supplied, so these are wonderful for working with non-parallel surfaces and objects. Sizes vary: most common today are 4" to 14", but larger ones are available, going up to 24". Rotating the handles quickly opens and closes the jaws and using the front screw for initial sizing works quickly, while the final pressure is applied with the rear screw. Jaws must be kept clean and free of glue drippings—a bit of masking tape over each jaw is a big help when the glue-up seems likely to be messy. Some people prefer to tape a piece of rubber or plastic in place over the tips, in order to prevent glue build-up. Such tip covers are reusable if cared for and cleaned and stored.

Band Clamps

One of the more useful clamps for round or octagonal or similar shapes is the band clamp. These clamps range from the light to moderate duty 1" wide bands, to bands 2" and more wide with heavy-duty screw adjusters to draw them up very tight. The bands are heavy nylon or canvas, and heavy-duty types can apply as much as 2,800 pounds per square inch of pressure. Shorter, lighter duty bands are usually about 10' long, while heavier duty types may be twice that long, or longer.

One-Handed Clamps

Some years ago, Quick-Clamps arrived on the scene, and were very quickly accepted as useful in hobby shops of all kinds. The reason was, and is, simple: the clamps' design allow the user to slip it closed and clamp it down with one hand, while the other hand could be occupied with holding the construct being assembled in place, together, or something similar. Popularity has remained high, and a few new developments have popped out over the years, including tiny clamps, 6" long, for light duty work, and spreader clamps for doing repair jobs such as removing and replacing chair rungs and splats. Now, American Tool Company is not the only maker, with Wolfcraft and others pursuing them heavily.

Spring Clamps

Spring clamps are useful for so many light clamping duties, it's hard to find a place to begin. You want either resin-bodied models like the Craftsman types from Sears, or steel-bodied types. Adjustable Clamp makes steel-bodied Pony models with openings from 1" to 4" (this is one big clamp, as it is about a foot long to give enough leverage to open that monster spring). Sears carries an array of plastic spring clamps that is exceptionally useful for light-duty uses, such as those found in birdhouse building.

Clamping and Clamping Pressure

Clamps are used for three reasons. Wood surfaces must be in direct and close contact with the glue; the glue must flow to a thin, continuous film; and the joint must be held steady until the glue dries. Clamping pressure varies with glue type, but usually suits glue thickness: the heavier the glue, the more clamping pressure. You need a thin, smooth glue line, not a joint squeezed dry, which may happen when too much pressure is used.

Most glues on softwoods fall in the intermediate thickness range, using clamp pressure of 100 to 150 pounds per square inch. Some dense hardwoods require pressures up to 300 p.s.i. Softwoods do not need a lot of clamp pressure. Deformation occurs with clamping pressures near 300 p.s.i. on softwoods.

A clamp may apply force ranging up to a ton. This pressure is divided by the total size of the clamped area to determine the pounds per square inch being applied. Home workers may occasionally apply too much pressure using hand-tightened clamps. This happens on large surfaces with closely arrayed bar clamps, but is not a frequent problem. Most of the time getting things aligned and getting clamps tightened firmly so that there is even squeeze-out is plenty.

Resorcinol and urea resins require a lot of pressure: epoxy needs little or none.

Always avoid excessive pressure in favor of even pressure over the entire area. Get even glue squeeze-out over the entire joint rather than racking the project up as tight as possible. The number of clamps any series of birdhouse project joints needs is variable; some people use very few clamps, others use far more. I use clamps every 8" to 10" with standard clamp sizes, and some light clamps get spaced as close as 4". I try never to space clamps more than 16" apart. If an item is only 6" to 10" long, I may use two clamps.

Corner clamps can hold joints together while the joints are worked on as well as while they are glued.

Brad nailers can often be used in place of clamps.

Use care in cutting, care in assembly, and care in glue application, and you will get a good and long-lasting joint if your selection of glue, or other adhesive, follows the preceding lessons. Glue is applied with a stick, brush, roller, or as the manufacturer directs, getting as smooth a coat as possible. This is done, on more complicated birdhouse projects, after a test or trial assembly, during which the clamps are set within a half turn of final adjustment. Clamp pressure is moderate, never exceeding about 300 p.s.i. so extreme force simply isn't needed. If you're turning clamp screws with pliers, you're working against yourself. Use enough clamps to get plenty of pressure without over-tightening any of them. Allow all glues and adhesives sufficient drying time—it's far better to leave clamps on too long than it is to remove them too early.

Mechanical Fasteners

Mechanical fasteners range from screws to nails and back again, with variations. If the variation isn't in the screws or nails, then it is in the devices to be used with them, such as hinges, lid supports, bracing, and mending plates.

Mending and bracing plates are simply flat metal plates that are screwed over a joint to brace that joint: they are often used on new joints as braces. Mending plates come in Ts, Ls, Hs, and other shapes that prove useful from time to time. They are made of solid brass, solid steel, and even plastic.

There are a number of types of wood screws and screw fasteners that are useful in building birdhouse projects, and for jigs that help us build birdhouse projects. Those that are most popular have become so for good reason. Today, new tools need new driver shapes, which require different head designs on the screws.

Many of today's screw types are meant to be power-driven: with cordless power drivers now on the market, cam-out (torque) resisting screws are needed more than ever. Cam-out is the twisting out of a slot or other style head (it is more likely with slotted screws) of the driver tip as power is applied. There's emphasis on Phillips head and square drive screws for use with both hand and power drivers. The new screws are adapted to use with hand drivers as well as power drivers.

Screw Types

Wood screws have round, flat, and oval heads, while metal screws mainly use pan, flat, and round heads. Commonly, wood screws up to about 4" or 5" in length and #16 in shank size are in most hardware stores, in a number of materials. Other sizes, and extremely small sizes such as ¼" x #0, #1, #2, or #3 may have to be ordered.

Wood screws are made of mild steel, coated or uncoated (zinc or galvanizing), solid brass, or stainless steel. Coated screws and solid brass are used where corrosion is a problem: a zinc or galvanized coating is

Brass or silicon bronze screws are best for birdhouse use.

normally used. Stainless steel screws are best when corrosion problems are extreme, such as on or around salt water (if you plan to keep any birdhouse projects made around salt water—on a boat, for example, use stainless screws instead of others). Steel screws are used where extreme strength is needed. Brass screws, weakest of the three commonly available wood screw materials, are decorative and corrode very slowly. In probably 85% of the cases, they're fine for birdhouse applications. Stainless steel corrodes hardly at all, but costs far more. Mild steel, even zinc-plated, is the cheapest and is seldom the best solution, as it will eventually rust.

Wood screws come in sizes from ¼" to 6" long. For screws to 1" in length, the step increase in length is ⅛", while screws from 1" to 3" long increase in length by ¼" at a step. Shaft sizes vary with length, with smaller shafts on shorter screws.

Power drive screws, fine and coarse threaded, come in sizes different than those used for other wood screws.

Power drive screws have a Phillips head or a square drive head. They are exceptionally useful for heavier uses, and for general light construction duties like those involved in building some of our larger birdhouse projects.

McFeely's washer head screws make it simple to build in removable bottoms and other parts. They remain on the surface of the wood and are easily loosened, tightened, and removed.

Screws are not as cheap as nails, but provide solid benefits for any extra cost. Holding strength is a lot higher. Disassembly is possible without destroying the project.

Screws are more work to install. For many screws, only a pilot hole is needed; for flat head wood screws, countersinking is also needed. Flat head wood screws are decorative, where screws are not meant to show, and are often counterbored as well as being countersunk. The hole is filled with a plug that may be flat to the surface or domed. The domed plugs are great for attaching wood roofing to birdhouses, as they automatically force good water run-off at what would otherwise be a weak point.

Drill pilot holes at least one size less than the screw shank in hardwood, and two sizes in softwood. Go half to two-thirds as deep as the screw will sink.

Other Screw Fasteners

A T nut is a type of nut that drive fits into a drilled hole in a wood surface. They are set in place and then tapped down so teeth in the upper ring grip. The screw is then run into the T nut, so assemblies mate. Ease of disassembly is built in.

Brass screw inserts work similar to T nuts as far as general installation, but are screwed into a hole drilled to size. Inserts have coarse male threads on the outside, and fine female threads on the inside. Brass inserts are screwed into the holes—tops are slotted to accept a standard flat-blade screwdriver tip. The insert is turned down until its top is flush with the board, after which a machine screw is driven into the internal threads. Knurled screws may be used, and are decorative. They also ease disassembly because no screwdriver is needed to install or remove them. I've used them a number of times for simple attachment of roofs to birdhouses, when the roof needs to be removable.

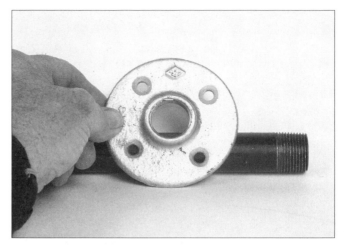

A plumbing floor flange fastened to the bottom of a birdhouse makes an ideal post mount for a threaded galvanized steel post.

Nails

Like the butt joint, the nail provides much woodworking fastening today. The nail is still one of the most useful mechanical fasteners.

Nails are sized by the penny, abbreviated d, a method once used by manufacturers to determine how many cents 100 nails would cost. Not a pound, but 100 nails. Given inflation over the past century, the actual costs changed, but the sizing system hangs on, ranging from 2d to 60d. Many makers now sell by length and weight.

Nails under 2d, or 1", are classed as brads; over 60d (6"), they're spikes. If you find a use for a spike in any of these projects, drop me a note.

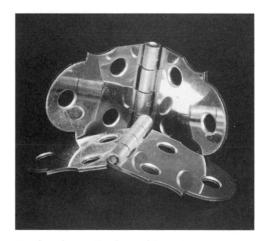

Stanley decorative brass hinges.

Common nails are used for general purpose nailing from framing work on through some types of flooring installation. Shank styles differ: for greater holding power use deformed shanks such as ring and screw. Coatings are available and nails may be hardened.

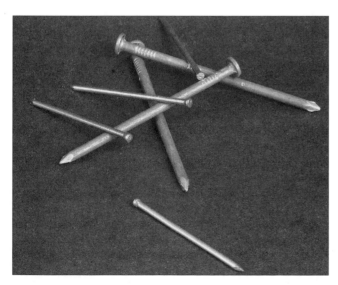

Common finishing nails.

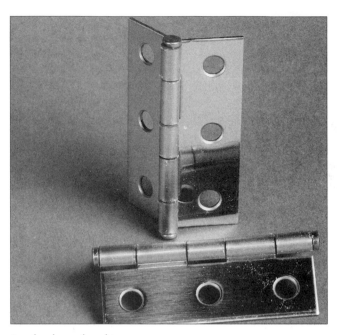

Stanley brass butt hinges.

Common nails come in aluminum and galvanized, for outdoor uses.

Box nails are like common nails, differing slightly in head size relative to shank size, with larger head sizes to shank diameters.

Finishing nails are slim, almost headless, in sizes from the 1" brad finishing nail on up to at least 16d (3½"). In mild steel, galvanized, and hot-dipped galvanized, they are used because small heads set easily (with a nail set) below a board's surface.

My primary comment about the use of nails for birdhouse building is that you may want to go with pneumatic nailers and their versions of nails. They are fast, the light-duty ones are easy and safe to use (keep your fingers out of the possible path of breakouts), and they create almost no bounce in materials, making precise placement a great deal easier.

Other useful items include plumbing floor flanges; hinges, both fancy and plain; screw eyes and hooks; wire; and a lot of bits and pieces that are readily found around most homes.

CHAPTER THREE
EXTERIOR FINISHES

The high sheen of a super-gloss clear finish is wonderful on pianos and patent leather footwear, but when building birdhouses, we're looking for something that doesn't glisten enough to startle birds, is easy to apply, and that protects as well—or better than—high-gloss finishes. Check out satin exterior finishes for clear, low-luster styles.

There are some basic similarities between finishes, but also some major differences, most depending on what the individual makers decide is the best combination of durability, ease of application, and appearance. Generally, ease of application is greater than durability on useful outdoor clear finishes. Appearance is always subjective, so you've got to judge for yourself what you like the most after trying a few types and brands.

Polyurethane gives a super sturdy finish, but needs UV resistance (as does any clear exterior finish, for otherwise, the film breaks down in less than a single season).

Selecting Clear Finishes

It is the selection of clear finishes that complicates the finishing procedure. Under normal circumstances, any good low gloss or no gloss exterior finish does very well.

Extreme warmth, as in summer, presents less of a problem than does extreme cold. Most finishes flow on decently in temperatures above 90°, and cure properly, but don't cure well below 60° even if they don't clump on the brush or rag.

Humidity is a controllable factor in shops and homes, but it is not always a factor that is controlled. For this reason, finishing all sides (top, bottom, both ends, and both edges) is recommended to reduce the exchange of moisture over the life of the furniture piece. The more coats, the better the reduction and the less effect moisture has on the wood parts of any project. Keeping humidity to rational levels within the shop—upwards of 35% and under 55%, for example—is fairly easy to do, but you retain no control of humidity once a project leaves your hands, so it makes sense to make it as resistant to airborne moisture as possible.

Prep: Clean, Dry Surfaces Needed

Make sure surfaces are clean, dry, and sanded to a smoothness available with a 150-grit sandpaper. The wide array of random orbit sanders available today take most of the grief out of fine sanding: they sand to a fine finish without leaving swirl marks, and reduce badly marred material to near perfection in a rush. Going beyond 150 grit is a waste of time in exterior applications.

Apply with a clean brush or a clean lint-free cloth. Give stain about 15 to 20 minutes to penetrate, and wipe off excess. For many jobs, you'll reach one end of the coating job just as you need to go back and wipe off the excess from the earlier parts of the work.

Let any stain used dry no less than six hours, preferably a dozen. If you want a darker color stain, lightly go over the surfaces with 0000 steel wool or 220-grit sandpaper, and repeat the staining process.

After twelve hours, you can safely figure on applying your first clear finish coating.

Clear finishes and the brushes you need to apply them (on the left is ZAR's spray-on exterior polyurethane).

Sand all edges to reduce splinters.

Porter-Cable's random orbit sander is a good choice for all birdhouse sanding chores.

Extra Coats

If you're going to apply a second or third coat on a piece the next day and are short of cloth for wipes, get a clean glass jar, place the cloth inside, and store it in the refrigerator overnight.

UGL's ZAR Exterior water-based poly is a finish that has worked well for me in a number of applications over the years. It gives excellent protection for exterior wood exposed to direct sunlight and the extremes of weather. It also has a good dose of radiation inhibitors to resist damage from ultraviolet rays. Among its other good points is the water clear-up, added to quick drying—recommended time to recoating is two hours, which means you can lay three coats a day on your birdhouse, and have it ready to go before you fold up and head out for the Saturday night movie. And it comes in satin, so you don't have to break a gloss finish with #0000 steel wool to get rid of glare.

Minwax makes several satin exterior products that are really excellent. Helmsman spar varnish is a clear finish, available in satin, designed for wood exposed to sunlight, water, and extreme temperature swings. Time to recoating is six hours, clean-up takes mineral spirits, and usually for best protection three coats are needed. Helmsman Spar Urethane has special UV absorbers to help restrain graying of the wood, while also protecting the wood from weather damage. Since it is a softer formulation than some other urethanes, it contracts and expands as needed to keep from breaking its film. Add to those Clear Shield, which gives a tough protection for exterior surfaces, again with UV absorbers to help prevent graying. Minwax calls it their most advanced current product for exterior wood protection.

Attention to Detail

Clear finish application is simple, but often messed up. Clean up carefully, and use a tack cloth, so there are no bits of steel wool left behind to create later rust problems and bumps in the finish. Modern safety directions say you shouldn't use a blast of air to clean out nooks and crannies in a project: use a good shop vacuum instead, and then use the tack cloth. Apply coats until you're satisfied with the finish, which shouldn't be more than three coats with exterior woodwork.

General Application Methods

Complete your birdhouse, right through hardware installation (hinges, lock pins, similar items on birdhouses). Remove the hardware. Use a one- or two-step sanding process: If wood is smooth to start, one step is fine. If wood is rough, use two steps. Start with 80 or 100 grit, depending on surface quality, as above; use 150 grit for a medium finish, which is all that's suitable for birdhouse construction. Vacuum the surface. Wipe down, very carefully, with a tack cloth. Apply the first coat of finish with a clean cloth made from an old T-shirt or diaper, a top-quality brush, or a spray system. Cover all sides and edges of the project with an equal number of coats. Lay on any successive coats the same way, allowing plenty of drying time (check the finish manufacturer's instructions). You can check both finish application for adequate coverage and see how much of the surface has dried by using a portable light placed at a low angle to the work surface.

You can use disposable brushes for painting. I did. This is from a package sold by Lee Valley.

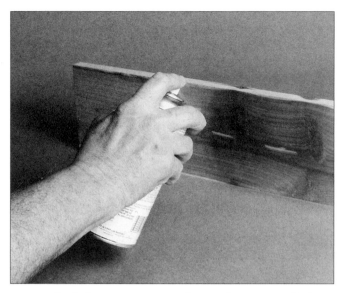

A spray finish from a can means fast application, and little or no clean-up.

Painted Finishes

Many birdhouses are improved by paint or enamel. While I've aimed at a casual look produced in part by design of the project, and except for one Victorian-style birdhouse, I've also used wood colors to produce the slightly vibrant, but dark feeling I've always gotten from that era. You may not wish to buy expensive and fancy woods, and may not have them on hand, so often plain pine does as well, especially if it's coated with an appropriate color in paint or enamel. Prepping a piece of wood to get a smooth coat of paint is essential, especially with enamels that are fairly thin and don't fill all that well.

Fillers

There are several choices in applying fillers. I usually use a sanding sealer to fill the worst surface whorls in the wood, then come back over it with a 180- or 220-grit sandpaper. Some woods, usually open-grain hardwoods like ash and oak, may require more work; you may choose to use an auto body filler on these. If you use the sanding sealer, two or three coats may be needed on some hardwoods. Bondo or its counterparts need one coat, wipe on, wipe off, and sand to 180 or 220 grit. Then apply the enamel, sanding lightly between coats with a 320-grit paper for finest results. For general birdhouse use, you'll probably not go beyond three coats

with little or no sanding between coats, especially with spray enamels such as Krylon, which dries so rapidly you can lay on successive coats at five- or ten-minute intervals. Brush-on enamels such as Red Devil are thicker, though still thin compared to most latex paints, and require fewer coats.

Start Your Prep

Start as if you're prepping for a clear finish, but sand to no more than a 150 grit. Apply sanding sealer (or body filler). Sand to 150. Apply the first coat of enamel and then let dry. You'll have an idea now of how much more sanding is needed, and how many more coats will be needed. Proceed as required, all the while keeping in mind you're building birdhouses, not formal furniture, and unless the birdhouses are being used for décor purposes, a super-high gloss is not a help in getting them occupied.

Eschew Complexity

Finishes are not complex for birdhouses. Here, you've got just about all you need to coat every one you ever build—and it is also possible to put birdhouses up in cedar, cypress, redwood, and other durable woods without any coating at all. The only time coating is necessary is when you use a wood such as pine or hemlock or fir.

CHAPTER FOUR
TOOLS AND THEIR USES

Hand tools needed for general birdhouse project construction include the claw hammer, hand saw, screwdrivers of a couple types, planes, chisels, miter box, nail sets, measuring tapes and rules, squares, levels, a brace and bit set, and clamps. You may add others, such as hand drill, push drill, protractor, and other items as you go along. Power tools can include nothing, or table saws, scroll saws, planers, jointers, routers and router tables, and a host of other tools. We'll look at some of those, and the general characteristics that make one more useful than another similar unit a bit later in the chapter.

Measuring Tools

Transferring measurements from plans to wood is basic to woodworking. Good-looking, long-lasting birdhouse construction depends on accurate measurements.

Measuring tapes come in many lengths and widths. For birdhouse project purposes, lengths above a dozen feet aren't needed, except for siting some larger projects. Get the best you can afford, with the widest tape available. The wider the tape, the stiffer it is, so the longer it lasts and the easier it is to read. At the same time, remember that a 20', 25', or 33' tape is difficult to control when making consistent 1" measurements along a 9" surface that is only 1" wide. A 10' or 12' tape is almost always best for birdhouse makers, and often a 6' tape is plenty, though most of those I've seen aren't much for quality.

The basics of measuring include adding a tilt to the tape or rule when a mark is made on the workpiece. The tilt gets the blade mark close to the surface, instead of as much as ⅛" in the air.

Accuracy is increased slightly . . . every bit helps. Get used to your measuring tools, and, even more important, if you're using one tape or rule to measure siting, use the same tape all through the job. Tape measures can vary as much as ¼" in a very short distance, and a quarter inch is enough to throw many projects so far off they never look right.

Marks may be made with standard pencils, carpenter's pencils, or scribes. A scribe is most precise, but the

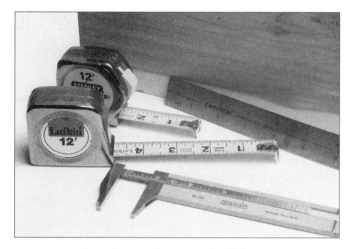

Two tapes and a caliper make up nearly all the measuring tools you need.

lead of a carpenter's pencil may be made nearly as precise, and makes a mark more easily seen. Cut the pencil down to a wedge, then sand the point sharp. Like many woodworkers, I keep a bunch of awls and scribes around, but tend to use pencils most, including standard pencils: keep a good sharpener around for these.

Use the shortest shank awl or scribe you can locate when marking, or pick up a marking knife. The knife actually gives the best line. Scribed lines are often easier to see in dark-colored woods—just tilt so the light hits the mark at an angle and you know where to cut.

Stanley's adjustable 6″ square works well for birdhouses.

An awl is a handy tool, as are any or all of these squares.

Marking gauges work well close to edges.

Measuring tools include rules and straightedges. Folding rules tend to be a bit unwieldy in the home shop, but some people still use them. I have a Veritas 24" aluminum straightedge, with a hardened edge that does probably 70% of my in-shop measuring work. It is accurate, easy to handle, and doesn't get lost as easily as all the other straightedges of lesser heft and length.

Squares

Squares of two types are useful in making birdhouses. The basic, or try, square is a rigid form of metal, or wood and metal. Blade length is 4" to 16" with or without markings. Combination squares offer many uses, from setting depths, to drawing rip lines to general square uses. Accuracy for most combo squares is lower than it is for top-quality try squares, though I do have a couple of Veritas(r) combination squares that are as accurate as any I've found, plus one cast-iron Chinese model that is quite good. Starrett of course is the best, but the price for a combo square is high.

Framing, carpenter's, and roofing squares are stamped metal Ls with a 2" wide blade and a 1½"-wide tongue. The long blade makes a good straightedge, but otherwise framing squares are not too useful for birdhouse making, until you reach owl- and duck-sized housing.

Work quality depends on squares and how well they're used; every shop needs a good combination square and a top-grade try square. The others are nonessentials that are sometimes nice to have.

Handsaws

Saws are the primary cutting tools for woodworking. For our birdhouse projects, nothing spectacular in the saw line is needed: a ten-point panel saw; a 12" or larger backsaw. For metal or harder plastics, get a hacksaw. For rougher cuts, one of the newer hard-tooth saws, with eight points per inch, works well, cutting quickly and neatly. These are the only low-cost handsaws I've seen that are worth what they cost. Actually, the newest

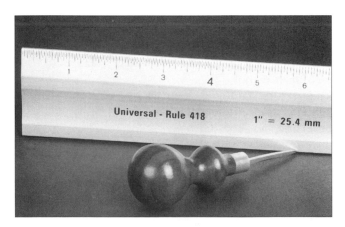

A good straightedge and a decent awl mean correct, clear marks.

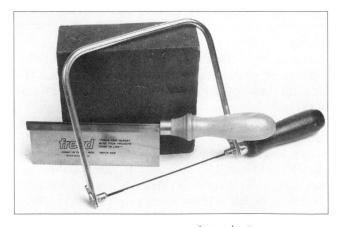

Vermont-American's coping saw and Freud's Gent's saw are good examples of very useful handsaws.

versions include some finish-cut saws that do a fast, clean job of producing cuts.

A hand miter box is a big help. For smaller-scale work, Jorgenson makes a couple of all maple miter boxes that have an extended front that hooks on the edge of your workbench. I've used one of these extensively in making small projects; it is great, low-cost tool.

Start a saw cut to the waste side of the line, guiding with the gripping hand's thumb knuckle against the side of the blade until the teeth bite. Cut with the handle at a comfortable angle, around 45°. Start with short strokes. When you get a good bite, then move a full arm stroke if space (and blade length) permits.

Saw care is simple. Make sure the blade won't strike the ground or other objects when wood is being cut. Make sure there are no nails in the wood. Don't force a saw that binds in a cut. Clean the blade; then try again. Often, a saw binds because the board is twisted. Handsaws must be hung up, not laid down. Keep the blade lightly oiled, free of gum and pitch build-up. WD-40 is a good clean-up tool, but not good for protection of more than a few days in any kind of humid environment. Use one of the proprietary protectors such as Top Cote.

Hammers

Hammers are available in many styles and sizes, but for our birdhouse projects, a good quality 16-ounce curved claw is fine as a general hammer, while 10- and 13-ounce hammers serve for light jobs. For light nailing, Vaughan & Bushnell's 10-ounce hickory handled small hammer does a superb job. Stanley and Plumb both make excellent 13- and 16-ounce models, with a variety of handle materials. Nailing balance with curved claws is better than with straight claws. The 16-ounce head is a good choice between lightweight and heavyweight (head weights vary from 8 ounces to 28 ounces). For birdhouse projects, get a 10- or 13-ounce model, unless you get a compressor and brad nailer.

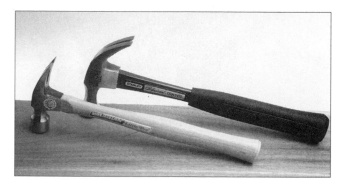

Stanley's lightweight hammer, at the rear, is 13 ounces. The Vaughan & Bushnell lightweight is 10 ounces.

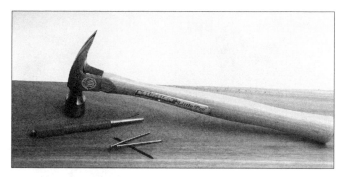

Vaughan & Bushnell's hammer is shown with a nail set and some finishing nails.

Handle materials include hickory and fiberglass as well as solid and tubular steel. There are advantages to each—wood costs a bit less and absorbs shock beautifully; fiberglass is easiest on the hand and forearm; steel is strongest. Make sure any hammer handle is securely attached to its head. Head weight is a personal choice, with standard weights ranging from 10 ounces (useful for much birdhouse project work) to a standard 16-ounce head, useful on many birdhouse projects. Bigger than that is not better.

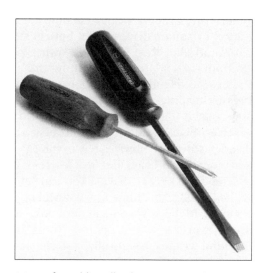

My preferred handle shape is a wedge.

Screwdrivers

Screwdrivers come in all the obvious head styles, to fit old and new head patterns. Select for head style and for quality. Good screwdriver handles fit your hand well, and blades are of alloys that last. Tip machining is clean and neat. For me, the best-handling screwdrivers are those with more or less cone-shaped handles that fit the hand better than do older, straight handles. The cones fill your hand to make getting a good grip easy. Newer models may also have a softer form of plastic for the handle, so your hand slips less.

Hand drills are a little harder to use, but also use more types of drill bits, and are a bit faster working than push drills.

To change the bit in a push drill, push the collar forward, remove the old bit, insert the new bit, and let the collar slide back. Drills—called points— are carried in the hollow handle.

Freud's Forstner style bits are good quality and available in sets.

Screwdrivers are frequently abused tools. Don't use yours for levers and awls unless you enjoy replacing them more often than is necessary.

For most uses, square drive works best, reduces torquing out to almost nothing, and is becoming ever more popular. Check the McFeely's catalog for the most extensive array of square drive screws, both in materials and sizes, around. Jim Ray, McFeely's owner, presents screw sizes from #4 x ⅜" to #14 x 4" (and that's just in flat head steel sizes). He also offers round washer heads, trim heads, self-drilling screws, statuary bronze-plated screws, brass-plated flat head screws, zinc-plated screws in several styles, black oxide platings, oversized round washer heads, stainless steel screws, silicon bronze screws, and even solid brass flat head screws (all the preceding screws are square drive). You can get a catalog at 1-800-443-7937, or online at www.McFeelys.com. You'll see a lot of McFeely's screws in this book, including my outdoor favorites, silicon bronze (boat building screws withstand weather beautifully) and stainless steel.

Match tip size to inset style and size and apply a twisting motion. Shank length is a matter of job requirements and preferences. As a basic recommendation, it is wise to go with a reasonable length shank, say 6" to 8", as these are the easiest to control.

Hand Drills

You may or may not be interested in hand drilling. With today's array of cordless drills, almost no one bothers with hand drills. At the same time, push drills and hand drills are excellent ways to get a few pilot holes drilled quickly without any worry about batteries or extension cords. The Yankee push drill, 03-046, has four drill points, with the largest ¹¹⁄₆₄" in diameter.

In addition, bit braces provide top nonelectrical means for drilling larger holes (up to 1", and to the limits of expansive bits, which go out to 3").

Drill Bits

A good-quality brad point drill bit set is a need. Brad point bits come in sizes from ³⁄₁₆" to 1" in most sets. Brad points allow easy starting without center punching, and the bits cut a nice, clean hole that is ideal for doweling.

For birdhouse work, consider Forstner bits. These bits cut an exceptionally clean hole and also produce a

Milwaukee's Power Bore bits are great for larger entry holes, but require more care to use as they'll tear the back out of a hole very easily. Use a very tight backerboard.

Hole saws also do a good job of cutting entry holes.

flat bottom in the hole. Forstner bits used to be expensive, and the top-quality ones still are, quite probably the most expensive wood bits. For clean work, they're worth it. Sizes go up past 3" but do not go down under ¼" because of bit configuration. Forstner bits do not get rid of heat too well because of their heavy heads, so must be run at slow speeds and work best if backed off and cooled down on deep holes. Also, most versions of the Forstner bit do not have much of a starting spur: cutting starts with the blades at the edges. This makes centering of holes fairly difficult.

For general small hole drilling, twist bits are the cheapest option. These Vermont-American bits are titanium-coated, which makes them a wee bit slicker to use in metals, but doesn't do much in wood.

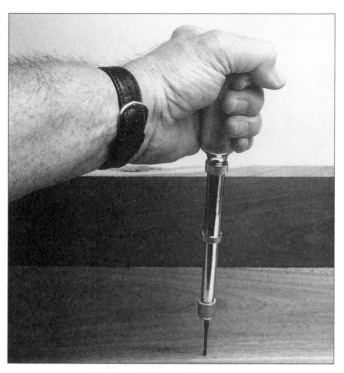
Using a push drill is near total simplicity: place the bit where the hole is to be, push down, relax, push down and repeat until you're through.

Spade bits are for rough drilling. The bits are cut from flat steel plate about ⅛" thick, and have spurs sharpened to give them a good bite. They cut fast, and they cut rough. Sizes generally run from ¼" up to about 1½" or 2". Keeping them sharp is easy and helps you get the best work from these bits. Dull spur bits tear wood badly.

To get the best use from any drill bit, when drilling through holes, clamp or otherwise fix a backing board where the drill bit will exit the wood. This reduces splintering, giving a clean hole. This technique works with any drill bit, but is most important when you're using spade bits.

Hole saws are not really drill bits, of course, but do cut neat holes in many sizes, and do a neater job than spade bits at about the same (fast) speed. They're readily available in sizes up to 6" diameter.

Power Tools

Stationary power saws provide great versatility in cutting, with the accuracy edge to the table saw, a tool that is as versatile as the router. Table saws come in a wide range of types, sizes, and styles, some light enough in weight to be moved easily from one job to another, others not easily moved at all. As with so many other woodworking tools, there is a plethora of options, and you should be able to readily suit your needs and budget pretty accurately. There's not much sense buying a cabinet saw, if all you'll ever do are projects similar to most of our included projects. At the same time, some of the super-cheap table saws are inaccurate enough to make good results darned near impossible. Choose first for size, next for accuracy, and last for weight, considering cost as it applies to your birdhouse building. If you are going further in woodworking, or already have, a router is a great tool. It is not needed for basic birdhouses, though, unless you decided to do some fancier edging on the boards.

Black & Decker's cordless driver/drill.

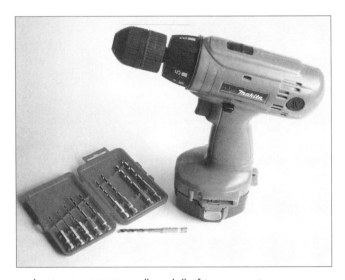

Makita's 14.4 NiMH cordless drill. If I were getting a new one, I'd go for the NiCad or the lithium batteries. The self-discharge feature of NiMH batteries is a nuisance with tools.

That's about it for table saws, as every project in here can be easily made without one. You'll see several models in our photographs, and can make a good online start to checking those out for yourself.

Routers

One of the most useful joint and edge producing tools we have is the router. Routers are truly one of the most useful woodworking tools you're going to find. You can produce any number of joint styles including fancy dovetails with one, and go on to produce raised panels for cabinetry. You may next run out all sorts of plain and fancy board edges, and you can even make your own molding in innumerable patterns. If you don't have a router, and expect to continue woodworking, buy one.

For general woodworking use, such as making birdhouses, pick a model with at least one horsepower, preferably with an adaptable collet to take both ½" and ¼" bits: the smaller collet does in most work: larger collets (⅜" is also available with some routers) are sometimes unaffordable, and the bits more expensive. The ¼"-collet-chuck diameter makes for slightly less accurate machining, something that's not of overwhelming importance in edge routing, though it can be very important in fancier work.

A plunge router is handy, though far from essential for most work. Routers on the market today offer more features and power than ever before. Power ranges from ½ to over 3 horsepower. For most home uses, a quality router offering 1 to 2 horsepower serves for years. Lighter duty routers are too limited for some work, while heavier duty models, those of three horsepower and more, are heavier and harder to handle, though they can really turn out heavy work. For birdhouse making, you need about a 1½-horsepower router.

Routers produce many types of joints, but for birdhouse making, they're handiest for edge shaping, making sure edges are rounded over and splinter-free.

Router bits cover an ever-widening range of shapes and sizes. Mortising and straight bits make similar cuts, but differ in important ways, with the mortising bits running cooler because of the different shapes. Edge and other molding bit patterns come in shapes and sizes that, today, seem limited only by the designers' imaginations.

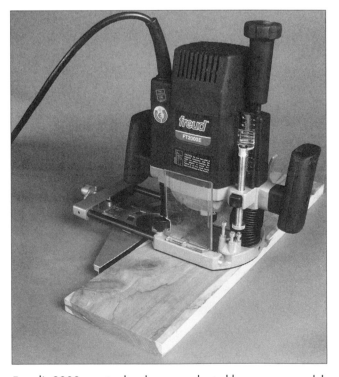

Freud's 2000e router has been supplanted by a newer model, but is a good example of heavy-duty plunge routers.

The router bit array is still growing, and each newly designed and produced bit adds slightly to the overall usefulness of the router, as do various router jigs and accessories. For this book, I stuck with a couple of routers and a router table from Bosch that accepts most Bosch routers.

Router Tables

Router tables are essential for the widest router use, and greatly extend precision and possibilities. A good router table turns a router into a small shaper (not so small in the case of some heavy-duty routers, and new, huge router bits that turn out panel work in sizes very close to those produced by production wood shapers).

You are no longer forced to design special jigs for each action: just use the table fence to position the work. Complex edging and molding parts for projects are more easily made, because cut depths are more easily maintained.

A good router table is an addition to be desired.

some sounds. Look for an EPA (Environmental Protection Agency) noise-reduction rating (NRR) of at least twenty-five decibels (db). For this book, I picked up a pair of bright yellow mouse ear types from Lee Valley (www.leevalley.com), and find they work exceptionally well. They're light, comfortable, and new pads are readily available when needed.

For dust-producing projects, use a dust mask. Disposable dust masks are good for keeping dust and fine solid particles from being inhaled. Some masks have a filter pad and holder with a strap to hold the mask over the nose and mouth. Others are formed shapes of filter material.

Safety glasses, goggles, and face shields must meet ANSI (American National Standards Institute) Z87.1.

Protect eyes, lungs, and hearing while woodworking, and use standard and common sense safety rules as well, adding the injunction to make sure the router remains in or on the work until the bit stops turning after the switch is turned off. If that uncovered bit is not moving when it touches you, it only makes small cuts.

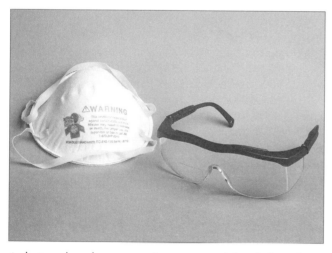

A dust mask and eye protection are essential tools for safety.

This DeWalt slide compound miter is a 12″ instead of 10″ and cuts thicker wood.

Lung, Hearing, and Eye Safety

Eye protection must always be worn while working with routers, whether it's safety glasses, safety goggles, or a face shield. I can personally attest to the simple fact that certain woodworking machines quickly ruin hearing. Among the worst are small planers, routers, and some vacuum cleaners.

Loud jobs require hearing protectors: most power woodworking jobs come under that heading. Hearing protectors help to prevent high-volume, high-frequency sounds from damaging the eardrums. The longer you are exposed, the more harmful those sounds are. Both insert and muff-type protectors are available. Insert-style protectors are found either in disposable form or in reusable molded styles. Muff-type hearing protectors are plastic cups filled with foam or liquid to help block

Compound Miter Saws

With proper saw set-up (mainly, support for longer boards so they don't twist and lift the saw off the work-table), power miter saws speed work and remove complexity from angle cuts—and from straight-end cuts. Most lumber doesn't make it to the shop with dead square ends, so a power miter saw set up to handle the work can shave the end of every piece, making sure you work from a square starting point. Newer SCMS (slide compound miter saws, the saws with the widest cuts) are exceptionally handy for making birdhouses, and prices have dropped in recent years. The first big SCMS were in the $1000+ range. Today, better saws can be had for half that, and excellent ones for still less.

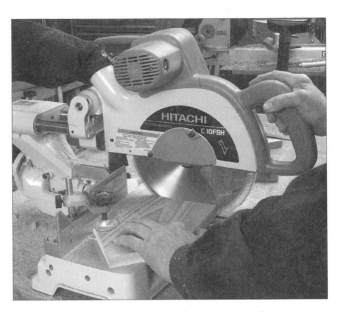

Using a Hitachi slide compound miter saw makes angle cuts very, very simple. Here, I'm starting the cut on the second of a front and rear pair.

Here, I am separating the martin house eave ends.

Cutting miters is far simpler with this type of miter saw than with any other. You will have no more difficulty lining up the cuts with a hand miter saw, or with a handsaw or circular saw, but you don't get the ease with the first two, nor the accuracy with the latter two that a power miter saw gives. And it's much easier, with a power miter saw, to slice off less than a blade's width at a time, shaving the edge to "creep fit" parts, making sure everything comes out perfectly. The saws are ideal for cutting eaves on birdhouses. In making these birdhouses, I used a Bosch 12" SCMS, a Hitachi 10" and a DeWalt 12".

A compound miter saw replaces a radial arm saw in the woodworking shop because the compound miter saw is simpler to adjust, stays in adjustment much longer, and is safer to use. You can make bevel cuts in material up to 12" in width with any of the slide compounds, and you can make miters in pieces to 8" wide. With some of the new dual compound saws, you can make right or left angle cuts at 60°.

An especially nice quality is the lack of climb in slide compound miter saws. A radial arm saw blade pulled through has a tendency to climb into that cut and create too fast a feed—this is dangerous and also chews up the workpiece. The slide compound miter saw pushes through the work, eliminating any tendency to climb, thus producing a cleaner cut.

There are quirks to many of these saws, and some are easier to use than others, so handle the one you intend to buy, or make sure the store has a liberal return policy (regardless of whether or not the store is mail order, a reasonable return policy on costly tools is essential for the buyer's protection).

Prices

Compound miter saws come in two basic styles, each with features that make it worth considering for those alone. You rapidly reach the point of needing to compare what the saw will do for you, in your own work, regardless of what it does for me, or your neighbor, or your best friend. When a tool's price goes over $200 (and many of these saws double that mark), it is time to consider the purchase carefully, thinking of the use the tool will get now and in future projects, and the effect the expenditure is going to have on your household budget. If you're lucky enough to have a hobby budget, one of the top-slide compound miter saws can wipe out a major part of your tool allotment very quickly.

Ease of Use

Look for ease of use of all controls. Everything from the safety button on the switch to the clamp for the stock being cut should work smoothly and easily for your hands. The adjustments should be easily made, with the head of the saw swinging through both its bevel and miter arcs smoothly. Preset stops should be accurate and should include 0°, 22½°, 30°, and 45°. Settings for crown molding should be clearly marked and easy to set to . . . this is less important if you expect never to use the saw for crown molding, but the capability is handy.

Also check the blade. The smoother cutting the better (for a 10" blade a 60-tooth blade with a 5° negative hook works well, while 80 teeth and the same hook work fine for 12" blades). Understand this, too: 12" top-quality blades cost a good deal more than 10" top-quality blades. Another point to be considering is intimidation: no one likes to think of a blade zipping along at 4500

RPM, give or take, 3" from his hand, but the 10" blade is less intimidating (though probably no less dangerous).

You can reasonably expect any of these tools to give you smooth-as-glass cuts if they're set up properly from the factory, or in your shop, and then a top-quality blade is used.

Because of the absolute need for ease of use with any of these saws, if you are ordering by mail, check carefully on the store's return policies. It is fair that you pay return shipping if you dislike the way the saw handles (assuming the poor handling isn't a matter of the quality of a particular example of the saw), but you don't want to also get stuck paying for a restocking fee. Ask first.

Weight and Portability

Weight may or may not be of importance. If you are not transporting your compound miter saw, it isn't important. Like any other tool of this type (table saw, radial arm saw), it suffers from transport movement, going out of adjustment more often when moved frequently.

Portability may be a more important factor to you than to others. If that's the case, pay attention to weight.

Lasers

Everything today has a laser on it. Compound miter saws are no exception. I've got two here now with lasers, and have had two others that I considered worth having. All of these are fairly costly saws, but the lasers are well integrated, and work nicely in a shop for marking the exact point of cut. They're not so useful outdoors on a bright, sunny day when the laser beam tends to be overwhelmed (dark glasses to enhance the laser beam are available, but usually don't fit too comfortably).

Jigsaws

Whether you call it a jigsaw, saber saw, or bayonet saw, the basic jigsaw can be a working tool or a waste of money, depending on a couple of things: you must have a need for cutting larger than ordinary circles (over the size you can cut with, for example, a 6" hole saw), curves, or arcs. If that's the case, buy something other than the cheap consumer models that vibrate you half to death and splinter even solid wood so badly the cuts look as if they were chewed by a demented beaver.

Several companies present two top-of-the-line models, one with a barrel handle and one with a loop, or D, top handle. Over the years of using jigsaws many migrate from one handle type to another: the barrel grip is easier to control on some cuts, but for most work—and for most precise work—having the hand directly over the blade is preferable (or so it seems to me). The barrel grip works better for those with larger hands as it tends to be fatter than the top handle grips. With some exceptions, though, manufacturers have a really mean

Jigsaws can replace my use of a band saw for cutting curves and designs. This Bosch is classed as one of the best made.

tendency to add speed dials to the trigger switches on top handles, which makes such switches uncomfortable to use. Lock-on buttons with most top handle models can present problems for some left-handed people who haven't adapted to the right-handed world: it's too easy, a couple of left-handed friends tell me, to leave the locks on when you think you're shutting them off. Fortunately, for all except the least adept, jigsaws are not the most dangerous tools in the woodshop, so some basic and rational care eliminates even the possibility of problems (primarily, keep your fingers away from the blade when the saw is plugged in, a good idea for any power tool with a blade or cutter). The blade on a jigsaw, like the bit on a router, is exposed, thus is dangerous, but it is nowhere near as dangerous as the much faster and sharper router bit. Woodworking tools meant for changing wood shapes are by definition dangerous, because anything that cuts wood will also cut flesh, and usually, bone. So use some common sense, and don't mess with moving blades or cutters.

Useful Brands

Bosch, DeWalt, Festo, Milwaukee, Makita, and Porter-Cable all offer models with varying degrees of extra convenience built in. The motors on these small saws are growing, and have just about reached the point on the power curve that was recently occupied by reciprocating saws, which are now getting close in power to where low end circular saws live. The most powerful, at least in ampere draw, is six amps. The next powerful isn't much below that—at 5.95 amperes.

Overall, it's hard to dislike any of the top-line jigsaws, especially if one grew up using the jigsaws around for both commercial and consumer use in the early '60s. Until more recent heftier units, jigsaws were a stepchild of woodworking, and deservedly so. You used one if you had to, but you didn't expect much, which was exactly what you got. These newer saws are all sturdy, weigh a lot more than you might think (several weigh over six pounds), and have cords 8' to 16' long. You don't have to worry about the plug hanging up as you cut a large arc or circle in that same sheet.

Overall, vibration is way down for the saws as a group; even the worst of today's saws vibrate much less than good models of the past. Cuts are easily carried out in various woods. Wood thickness, assuming the blade reaches through the material, slows the cut slightly in hardwoods, but otherwise isn't a problem.

Tool-Free Blade Changes

Toolless blade changes are possible with several of jigsaws. Tool-free base changes are available on a few.

In general, it's reasonable to say there is good quality out there for the buying. One thing is for sure: if you use any care at all in making your selection, you should get a jigsaw that will serve as well or better than any that have gone before.

A jigsaw can save the sometime woodworker the cost of buying and setting up a band saw. It isn't as accurate, but can handle most of the same cuts at a far lower cost, and in much less space.

More Tools

There are many more woodworking tools to be considered if you're going beyond birdhouse building, or even if you're staying with birdhouses and producing more, or producing more complex, birdhouses. For the most part, though, and with the exception of band saws and scroll saws, the preceding section pretty well covers it all as far as absolute essentials go.

Scroll Saws

The modern scroll saw is a wonder to use. The mid-range models, such as the DeWalt and Delta models, are close to vibration-free, cut very nicely indeed in their designated cutting classes and are easy to set up and maintain, with fast and easy blade changes. Both the above models come with blowers and can be had with accessory lights—the Delta comes with its own stand, but the stand is an extra option on the DeWalt. A couple of the plans in this book have some modified Victorian-look scrollwork: a good scroll saw does this in no time, while a coping or fret saw takes forever (and is harder to use well). The quality of blades is truly important with scroll saws. Go for the best you can find. I've been using Olsen blades for some time, and have had excellent results.

Band Saws

A good band saw makes a great many chores much easier. Band saws are great for cutting curves in materi-

The band saw is a bit smoother to use than the jigsaw, but is another tool cost you may not need if you already have a good jigsaw.

al too thick to allow use of a scroll saw, and also do sweeping large curves much more easily. In addition, they can be used for pattern cutting or sanding—in this method, you tape as many pieces of wood together as you need, and cut or sand them all at the same time (sanding "blades" are available for many band saws). This saves time for anyone making more than one of a single pattern, and most full-sized (14" and larger) band saws can cut at least seven pieces at one time, in almost any kind of wood. Large band saws with taller capacities can cut more. Resawing is another favored job with band saws. It requires some time to learn to do well, but is the safest and easiest way to reduce the thickness of boards, without using a planer.

Planers & Jointers

With the advent some years ago of the portable planer (Ryobi's AP10 was the first), affordable planing was available for the home hobby shop without major financial sacrifice. Today's versions have increased in size, with 13" being a common width, stayed about the same price, and added many new features—the new Ryobi 13", for example, has a slide across head lock to reduce snipe. It is the easiest-to-use head lock I've seen yet. Fast re-set turrets and a host of new features, including quick change blades, make these planers more useful than ever before. Once you've been told that, you have to sit down and figure out if the ability to thickness woods fairly quickly and very accurately is of great importance in your work. You'll find planers especially useful if you choose to buy unsurfaced wood, which is a great way to save money (buying green, unsurfaced wood can reduce wood costs up to 60% over time). If you build only a few small projects a year, a planer is a waste of money.

Jointers are seldom a waste of money. A small, high-quality jointer helps you make tight joints on almost

This planer is thicknessing red oak.

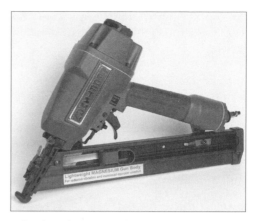

Pneumatic finish nailers use a thicker nail 15-gauge versus 18-gauge—compared to brad nailers. If you use the bigger nailer, be careful to stay back from edges where it may split boards.

any project of almost any size. Large jointers help make tight joints on larger projects as well as on smaller ones. Generally, 6" jointers are considered suitable in size and cost and utility for most home workshops.

Pneumatic Assembly Tools

How many times does hammering away to glue and nail light projects of odd shapes produce nothing more than a bouncing assembly that quickly becomes a pile of sticky bouncing parts? Or how often do you have 100 or more slender nails to go into a project, or series of projects, nails that must then be set and the holes filled and sanded. Or you wish to fasten a backboard on a rabbeted cabinet or case back without using glue.

The list is not endless, but is extensive. There are a great many projects that we wish to assemble with nails, and many of those, from tiny to huge, require an approach that is easier to use than even a 13- or 10-ounce hammer

Craftsman's pneumatic brad nailer took part in every one of these projects, to good effect.

and a nail set. There is a cure for bouncing around on the bench top, and for pounding in multitudes of finishing nails that must be set. Air finish nailers set nails as they drive them.

The tool of choice for the above jobs is the pneumatic, or air, fastening tool. For woodshop use, there are three versions that serve about every purpose that's ever going to come to the assembly bench. A further type, the framing nailer, is a great one, too, but unless you do a lot of heavy outdoor furniture building, or much shop framing or other structural work, it's not a need for the average woodworker, any more than the timber nailer, driving 5⅛" fasteners, is essential to Joe or Jane Homeworker.

Firing Operation

The nose is placed against the work, and the trigger is pulled, and the tool will not refire until the nose is removed and replaced against the work. Handy. No bounce.

For the average woodworker, the decision on which of the three finish fastening tool types to buy depends on the type of work done. If you make only modest-size projects, any of the brad nailers will do, as is the case if only glue-nail work is done, where the nail serves primarily as a clamp until glue sets. Birdhouses fall into this category.

Brad Nailers

The brad nailer is the lightest, easiest to use of any pneumatic fastening tool. These are the finish nailers of choice for most woodworking shops. They drive nails from as short as ⅝" up to 2" long, in an 18-gauge thickness that saves a lot of split wood in lightweight projects. I've been using two Craftsman brad nailers for some time now, and am completely satisfied with them. These small nailers can be driven with just about any air compressor made, as they require very little air to work. One of the nicest features of a brad nailer is the fact that the single-step driving of the brad means the project doesn't bounce around and semi-disassemble itself as you work.

Finish Staplers

Finish staplers give you the means of securely fastening backs onto projects, installing shingles on birdhouses, and of quickly assembling drawers. For the most part, woodshop needs for a stapler are well answered with a ¼"-crown-finish stapler, providing an easily hidden fastener that provides good holding power.

Lowering Wood Costs

Saving money by buying rough wood requires two things: first, patience; and second, access to a planer. Obviously, there's also some need for space where the wood can be stacked with its top covered. This is not a solution for the city-dwelling woodworker. It is also not a real solution to someone who doesn't have access to rough-cut wood.

A moisture meter is a handy item: the Lignomat I am currently using has a bottom measure of 6%, on a diode light, for lowest moisture level. Planing may take place when moisture levels drop to about 15%. You may plane wet if you wish, but it's a mess. Some hardwoods are difficult to plane on lightweight home shop planers, and wetness doesn't help at all. The Wagner shown in use here does a great job, too.

My lightweight planers do a fine job of planing wood, from pine to walnut, producing finish-planed wood. They must work harder with white oak, but will do the job, if you let them cool down after every 30 minutes of use. These are NOT production planers. If you treat them as if they are production tools, they'll wear out very, very quickly.

Birdhouse builders require relatively small amounts of lumber, unless you decide to produce major numbers for gifts or for sale, so the above advice may not apply to you. You can pick up cedar, cypress, and similar woods at reasonable cost at many woodworking stores, and by mail, S2S (surfaced two sides), and need only use a hand plane to smooth one side before ripping the wood to width. A power jointer does a much faster job of getting one side even and the board ready to be sawn so it has parallel sides.

There are a great many more woodworking tools available to you. With the basics covered early in this chapter, added to your personal needs and desires among the power tools quickly described, you can outfit any workshop to build any birdhouse you may want to construct, including fancy Victorian-style models and multiple-entry-type houses, useful for martins.

Porter-Cable's Quicksand random orbit sander. Random orbit sanders remove material quickly, but leave an exceptionally smooth finish, so are suitable for medium and fine sanding.

This is Wagner's pinless moisture meter. It works quickly and is accurate.

BIRDHOUSE DESIGNS

PROJECT ONE
BASIC BIRDHOUSE
for Titmice and Others

The basic birdhouse for titmice starts with selecting boards. We used pine for this version, and may paint it after its first season outdoors.

Materials:

1 piece ¾" x 6½" x 25" for front and back (one piece 8½" long, one piece 16¼" long)

1 piece ¾" x 4¾" x 23½" for sides, bottom

1 piece ¾" x 7½" x 7½" for top

1 brass butt hinge

1 brass hook and eye, 1" to 1½" in size

nails (brads), glue, and screws

paint, or clear finish, if desired

Basic Birdhouse for Titmice and Downy Woodpeckers

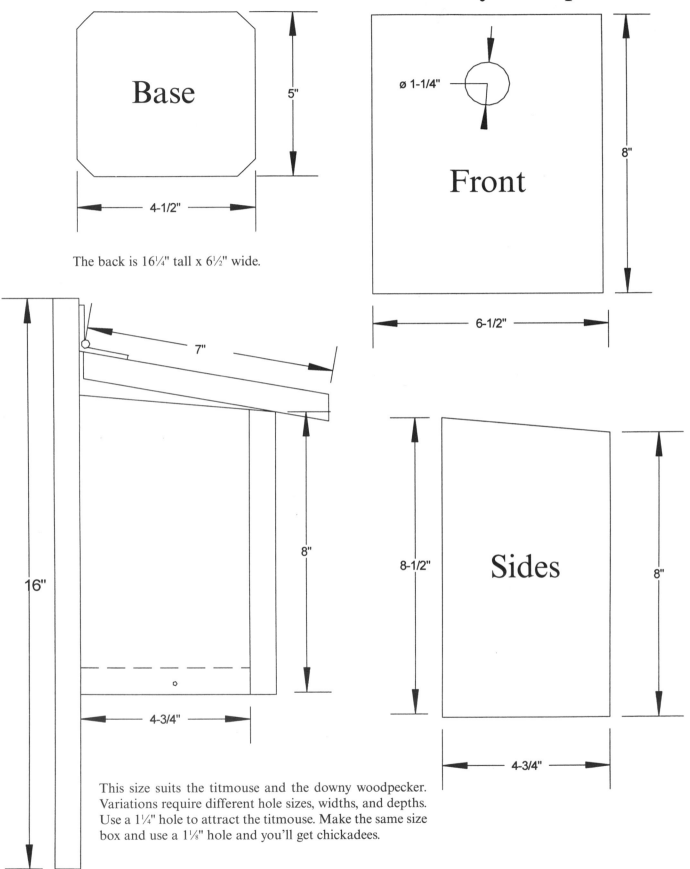

Base

5"

4-1/2"

The back is 16¼" tall x 6½" wide.

Front

ø 1-1/4"

8"

6-1/2"

7"

8"

16"

4-3/4"

Sides

8-1/2"

8"

4-3/4"

This size suits the titmouse and the downy woodpecker. Variations require different hole sizes, widths, and depths. Use a 1¼" hole to attract the titmouse. Make the same size box and use a 1⅛" hole and you'll get chickadees.

Ripping the pine board to width. Guard removed for photo clarity. It is best to work with guards in place. Start of rip.

Finishing the rip.

1. Rip the boards to the width on the drawing if they are not already to size—the front is 6½" wide, sides are 4¾" wide, and the back is the same width as the front. The roof is 1" wider to leave an overhang.

2. Bevel the roof board 10° at the back (the edge that fits against the back).

3. Cut sides with a 10° miter, front to back (the back is ½" taller).

4. Cut back to 16¼" length.

5. Cut front to 8" height.

6. Drill 1¼" hole centered on front and about 2½" down from the top edge. Use a Forstner bit, if possible. Use a tight, different-colored backerboard to eliminate splintering at the rear of the entry hole.

7. Cut the base 5" long off of material the same width as the sides. Clip edges ½" on each corner for drainage.

8. Place the back on the bench, and set all pieces in place to check cuts and sizes.

9. Place one side upright on the bench. Set the other side approximately the correct distance from that side, and lower the front in place, with the entry hole at the top—the mitered top edge of the sides should have the shortest side toward the front of the box to be formed. Check fit and remove front.

10. Mark for screws, and use countersink for the correct size screws (#6 x 1½" brass or silicon bronze). Place the parts as shown so holes are also drilled in the back to match those coming in from the front (this isn't essential, but eases the process).

Clipped corners allow drainage.

Testing fit is a good idea before starting assembly.

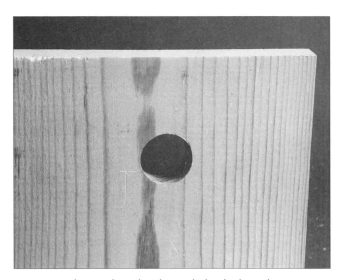

A Forstner bit makes drilling easy, and drilling through is visible when you see different-colored chips.

A Forstner bit combined with a tight backerboard gives a clean cut out on both sides of the hole.

11. You can use glue to make a solid seal along the edge, or simply screw the parts together. Start with one front edge, and place screws. Move on to the second edge and drive screws.

12. Place front facedown on the bench, and align the back so the holes are on the rear edges. Drive screws for one side. You may now have to twist the back or side to make them align properly. Much depends on the quality of the pine you've managed to find. In recent experience, most pine you'll find is apt to be badly cupped, split, or otherwise much closer to the kindling pile than it should be when sold commercially. Drive screws for the second side.

13. Align the roof—center it over the box, which should leave ½" overhang on each side—making sure you've got the beveled side at the back, and the short edge facing down onto the box. Mark the position for the hinge at the center of the roof and back.

14. Install the hinge on the roof and then install it on the back, maintaining the half-inch clearance on each side of the roof.

15. Install the brass hook and eye at the center underside of the roof and the front.

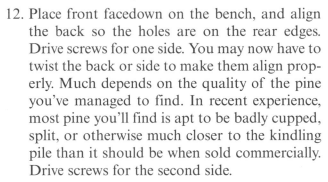

Drill marks from front show where next drilling is needed. Just barely touch the stacked board in back.

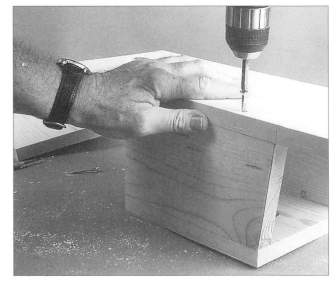

Installing the front first makes installing the back easier.

Install the hinge with the birdhouse lying on its side for easy gripping.

Remove hinge before spraying on finish. Reinstall hinge after finish dries.

16. Insert the clipped corner floor and drill pilot holes for the #6 x 1½" washer head screws. Insert the screws. A third screw can be added at the front if desired, which will keep the bottom from pivoting.

17. Remove the hinge, the hook, and the eye.

18. Sand carefully to no more than 150 grit.

19. Paint or spray on clear exterior polyurethane.

20. When the coating is dry, reinstall the hinge and the hook and eye.

Remove hinge before spraying on finish. Reinstall hinge after finish dries.

PROJECT TWO
BASIC BIRDHOUSE
for Bluebirds

This project is very similar to the first one, with slight size differences and a different fastening method. Cypress does a better job for this version and won't need paint for durability.

Materials:
1 piece ¾" x 6½" x 24" for front and back (One piece 15" long, one 8½" long)
1 piece ¾" x 5" x 23½" for sides, bottom
1 piece ¾" x 7½" x 7½" for top
1 brass butt hinge
1 brass hook and eye, 1" to 1½" in size
glue and screws
clear finish, if desired

Basic Birdhouse for Bluebirds

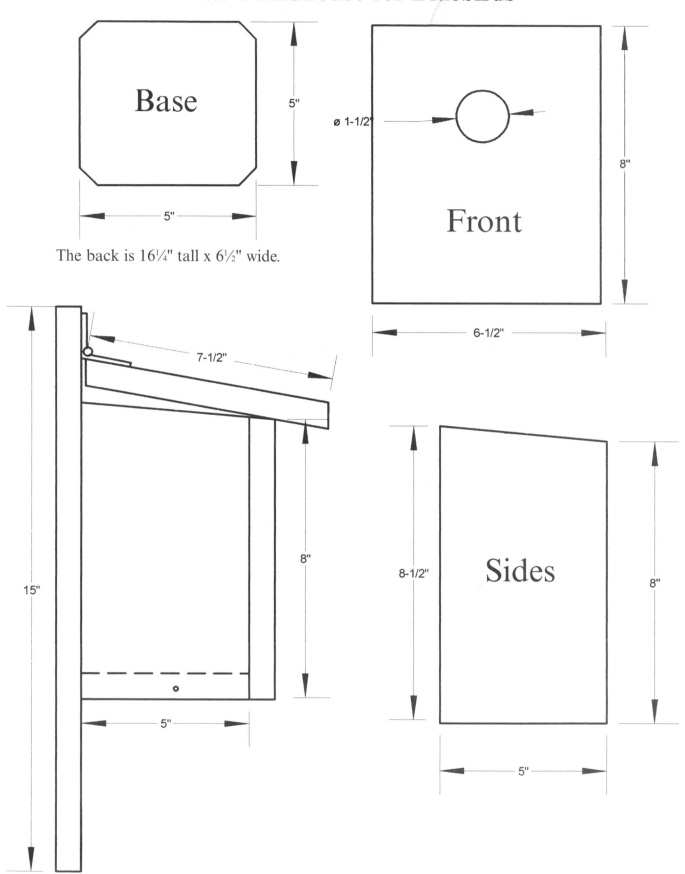

Base

5"

5"

The back is 16¼" tall x 6½" wide.

Front

ø 1-1/2"

8"

6-1/2"

7-1/2"

8"

15"

5"

Sides

8-1/2"

8"

5"

Starting drilling of entry hole.

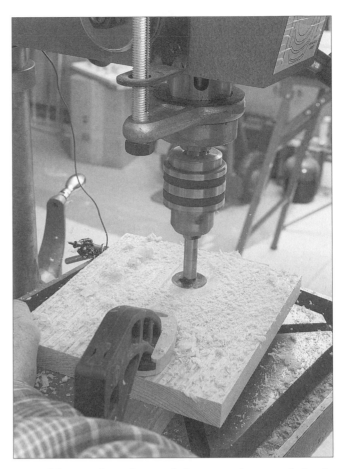

Most of the way through entry hole. Use a slow, steady feed with Forstner bits, and keep rotational speed down to under 400 RPM with this size bit.

1. Rip the boards to the thicknesses on the drawing if they are not already to size—the front is 6½" wide, sides are 5" wide, and the back is the same width as the front. The roof is 1" wider to leave an overhang.

2. Bevel the roof board 10° at the back (the edge that fits against the back).

3. Cut sides with a 10° miter, front to back (the back is ½" taller).

4. Cut back to 15" length.

5. Cut front to 8½" height, mitered to 8" at its front edge.

6. Drill the 1½"-entry hole centered on front and about 2" down from the top edge. Use a Forstner bit, if possible. A tight, different-colored backerboard eliminates splintering at the rear of the entry hole.

This birdhouse is made from cypress. Here, all parts are cut and being test-fit before assembly.

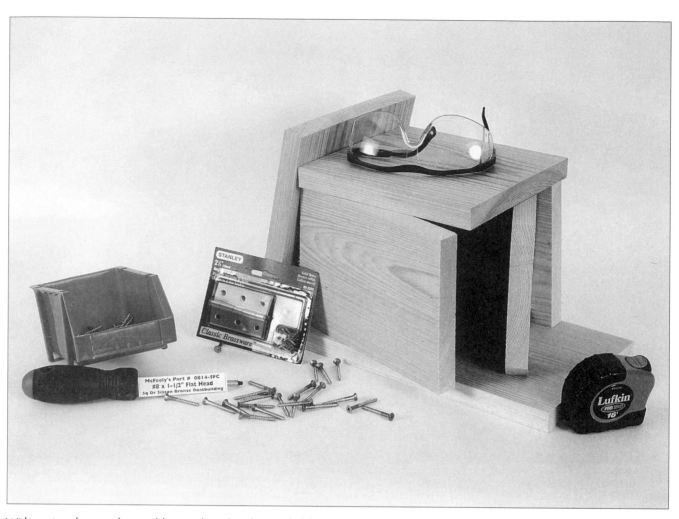

With cutting done and assembly tested, gather the needed fasteners.

7. Cut the base, 5" square, off of material for the sides. Clip edges ½" on each corner for drainage.

8. Place the back on the bench, and set all pieces in place to check cuts and sizes.

9. Place one side upright on the bench. Set the other side approximately the correct distance from that side, and lower the front in place, with the entry hole at the top—the mitered top edge of the sides should have the shortest side toward the front of the box to be formed. Check fit and remove front.

10. Coat edge with Titebond III, and drive brads to hold in place. Coat both sides of the joint with glue to get a good joint, as the three brads used do not add appreciably to the joint's strength.

11. Move on to the second edge, add glue and drive brads.

12. Place front facedown on the bench, and align the back (this is most easily done if you mark all the way around the spot where you wish to have the roof touch: leave about 1½" at the top front above the top of the roof). Things can get a bit sloppy here: use a brush to add glue to both back edges and to the back where it touches those edges. Place the back and drive brads in one side. You may have to twist a bit to align the other side, though with well machined cypress we didn't have to. Drive the brads for that side.

Here, the hinge is in place.

The roof latch is placed.

13. Align the roof—center it over the box, which should leave ½" overhang on each side—making sure you've got the beveled side at the back, and the short edge facing down onto the box. Mark the position for the hinge at the center of the roof and back.

14. Install the hinge on the roof and then install it on the back, maintaining ½" clearance on each side of the roof.

15. Install the brass hook and eye at the center underside of the roof and the front.

16. Insert the clipped corner floor and drill pilot holes for the #6 x 1½" washer head screws. Insert the screws. A third screw can be added at the front if desired, which will keep the bottom from pivoting.

17. Remove the hinge, the hook, and the eye.

18. Sand carefully to no more than 150 grit.

19. Hang the birdhouse, remembering that bluebirds do very well at fence-post height.

PROJECT THREE
VICTORIAN BLUEBIRD HOUSE

This is a break in the usual bluebird house tradition. At this point, I've built so many traditional bluebird houses, that a couple nontraditional plans seemed like a good idea. These houses do well, by the way, for both Eastern and Western bluebirds. The house is a bit fancier, takes a little longer to build, but still needs mostly lumber scraps. It is mounted either to a fence-post-high post with a plumber's flange (in which case, the house is unscrewed from its base and lifted off for cleaning), or is held by a screw driven into a wooden post through the 1½"-entry hole: two screws can fit, one at the top of the hole and one at the bottom. It's at this point that McFeely's 6"-long square drive power bit is really handy. The bottom may also be removed and a screw driven at a slight angle upward into a wooden post, instead of running two through the entry hole. Use only one, then.

Pine worked well here, with some narrower boards that weren't totally cupped, but we also used some white oak sides from scrap material that was lying around the shop.

Materials:

1 piece ¾" x 6½" x 22½" pine for front and back

1 piece ¾" x 5" x 18" pine for sides, floor (substitute oak or other wood as available).

2 pieces ¾" x 8¼" x 8" pine for roof

1 piece ¼" x ½" x 3½" for perch

2 pieces ½" x 2⅛" x 8⅜" trim pieces for side. Scrap exotic was used, but it's been around so long, no one knew for sure what it was.

paint: yellow for roof, blue for body of house

Victorian Bluebird House

Full-sized roof eave pattern
for Victorian birdhouse

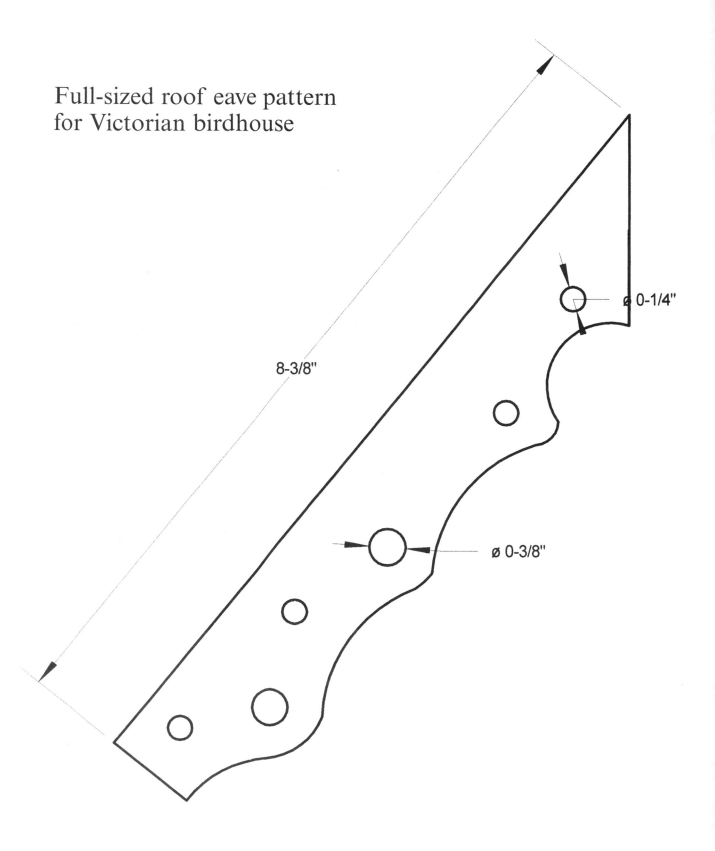

8-3/8"

ø 0-1/4"

ø 0-3/8"

Victorian Bluebird House

Cut upper roof edges to 40 degrees: 80 deg. total.

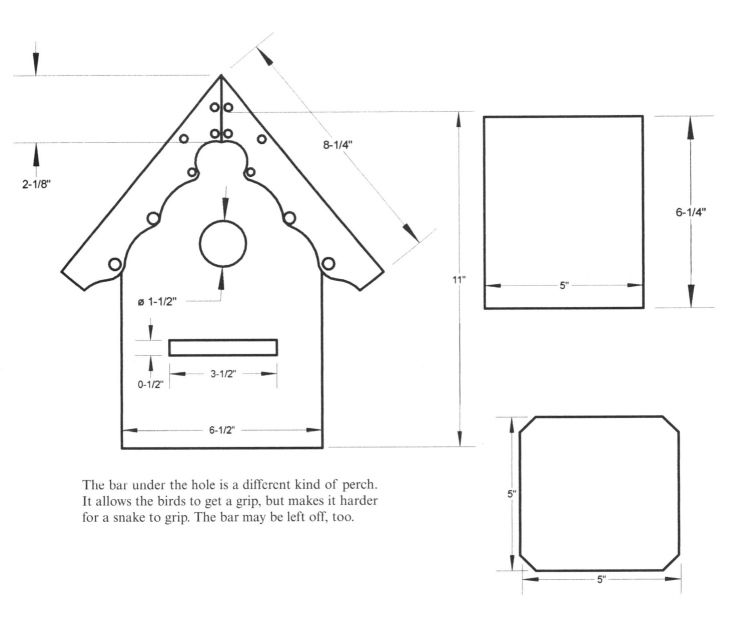

2-1/8"

8-1/4"

ø 1-1/2"

0-1/2"

3-1/2"

6-1/2"

11"

6-1/4"

5"

5"

5"

The bar under the hole is a different kind of perch.
It allows the birds to get a grip, but makes it harder
for a snake to grip. The bar may be left off, too.

Bottom is 5" x 5". Clip each corner
½" for drainage.

Cutting the first roof bevel at 40° is easy with a compound miter saw. The cut may also be made on a table saw, or with a block plane (but it is cross grain and more difficult to plane).

All parts except eave trim boards are cut and ready.

1. Cut wood to length, as above.

2. Cut front and back roof angles at 40° at each end of the 22½"-long piece. The easiest way to do this is to mark a line up the center on both sides of the wood, then set the saw to 40° and cut on side of the roof, using the center mark on that side. Flip and cut. Bring the other end around and cut one side. Flip and cut the other. The saw does not have to be reset this way.

3. Trim the top edges of the eave pieces while the saw is set to 40°.

4. Bore the 1½"-entry hole at about the level of the eaves for a centerline in the front—only!

5. Clip two edges off the end of the 5" length.

6. Cut a 5" length free of the long 5"-wide piece, making sure the clipped edges are on the cut-off piece. This is the floor, and you can now clip off two more edges.

Assembling the first side. Birdhouses go together more easily if you stand two sides up while nailing the first. The second side serves as a support. Use glue only on the side being nailed, though.

The second side is braced by the already nailed and glued first side. Note light glue squeeze-out, easily wiped off.

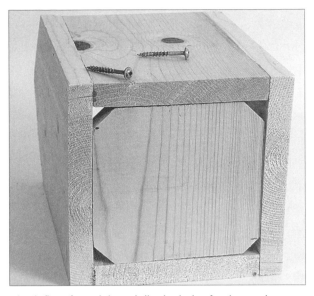

Check fit at back, and then glue both sides, slide the back into place, and nail both sides.

Check floor fit and then drill pilot holes for the washer screws that make the floor easily removable for clean-out.

7. Cut the sides to 6¼" long.

8. Cut the roof to a 40° bevel on one side, and then repeat on the second piece. Both roof pieces need to end up 8¼" long on the long side of the angle.

9. Place two sides upright and align the front on them. Lift the front off.

10. Place glue on *one* side, set the front back on the two sides, and drive three brads in the glued side to secure things until the glue dries.

11. Place glue on the second upright side, align the front, and drive brads.

12. Turn the front facedown, leaving the two glued sides standing up. Check fit of back. If all is well, remove the back, place glue on both sides, place the back and drive three brads per side.

13. Check the floor for fit. If it is right, drive a #6 x 1½" washer head screw through each side into the floor. Pilot holes are recommended here. A third washer head screw may be placed at the front to keep the floor from tipping, if it is needed. It can be added later after weather affects the birdhouse.

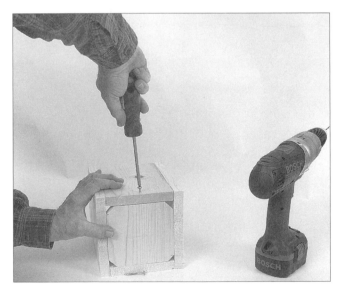

Bottom screws may be driven by hand or driver/drill.

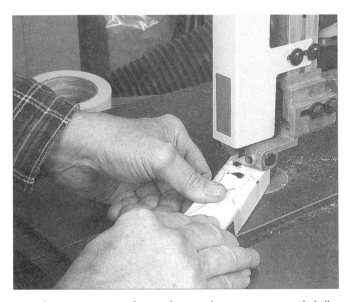

Tape the eave section plan to the sized eave cutouts and drill holes before starting cuts.

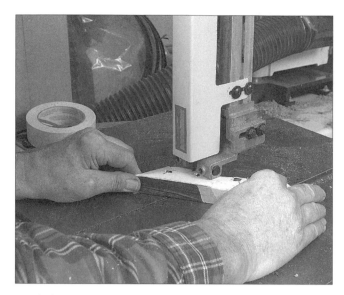

Finish the eave cuts while staying as close as possible to the lines.

The house structure is sprayed with dark blue Krylon.

14. Paint the birdhouse. We used Krylon spray enamel here, for ease of application. Try to keep paint off the eave edges.

15. Check roof angle fit. If all is well, align one side of the roof with half the overhang in front and half in back, after placing glue on the edges of the eave cuts on that side. Use three brads to position and secure the roof side until the glue sets.

16. Repeat with the other side.

17. Tape the full-sized eave pattern onto the taped together eave pieces. First, drill the decorative ¼" and ⅜" holes. Then cut out the pattern on a band saw, scroll saw, or with a jigsaw.

18. Sand the entire birdhouse lightly. Sand the eave parts lightly.

19. Place masking tape on roof front edges.

20. Coat the roof with paint. Two coats is a good idea.

21. Once the paint dries, remove the masking tape, place a few dots of epoxy on the edges of the eaves, and brand nail the trim pieces in place.

22. Install the ¼"-thick perch/support. Use ⅝" brads, and glue, but scrape the paint where you install the perch so the glue can get purchase on wood.

23. Hang at fence-post height.

Roof paint is a flat but bright yellow, for which I used craft paint that is supposed to be an indoor/outdoor variety. Two coats for long-term durability is a good idea.

PROJECT FOUR
WREN HOUSE

By definition, wren houses are small, which tends to make them easier to build in some ways, but harder to make unusual. A solid roof is needed, because wrens like to perch up, and are one of the few birds that accept a swinging nest site. We had some scrap purpleheart around the shop, so trimming the birdhouse with strips of purpleheart seemed like a good idea.

The roof is a simple overlay, with one piece cut ¾" longer than the other, mated at 90° with glue and brads. The roof is also made for a long overhang in front for no reason other than the feeling it looked good and protected against driven rain. The house itself is made of Eastern red cedar, milled locally.

Materials:
1 piece ¾" x 7½" x 4⅝" roof
1 piece ¾" x 7½" x 3⅞" roof
1 piece ¾" x 11¾" x 4½" front and back
1 piece ½" x 10½" x 3½" for sides and floor
1 piece ¼" x 1" x 20" trim (purpleheart used)

Wren House

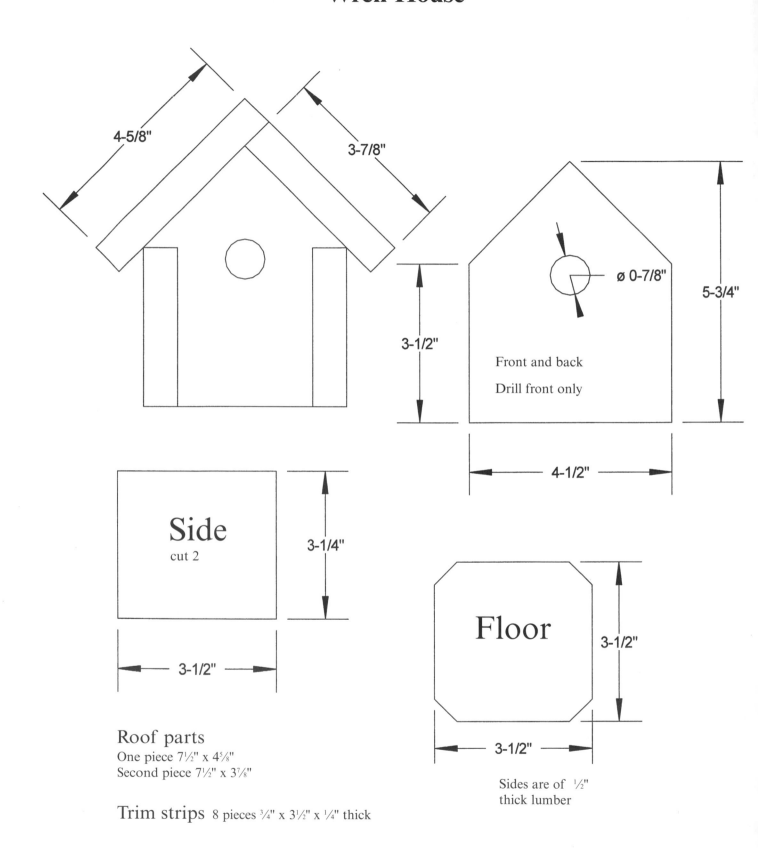

4-5/8"

3-7/8"

3-1/2"

ø 0-7/8"

Front and back

Drill front only

5-3/4"

4-1/2"

Side
cut 2

3-1/4"

3-1/2"

Floor

3-1/2"

3-1/2"

Sides are of ½"
thick lumber

Roof parts
One piece 7½" x 4⅝"
Second piece 7½" x 3⅞"

Trim strips 8 pieces ¾" x 3½" x ¼" thick

Check width of material for sides and bottom.

Square one end of material.

Start roof eave cut with plenty of material to allow hands to stay away from the blade. Compound miter saws are wonderful tools if used safely.

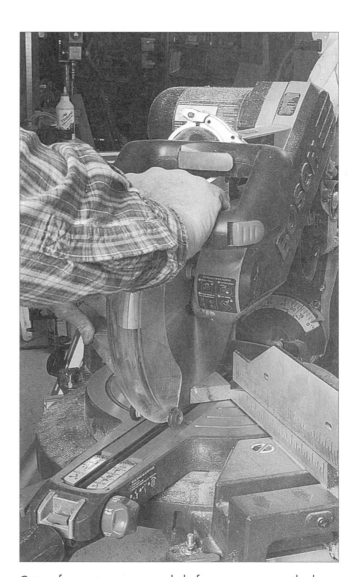

Cut roof eaves to correct angle before you separate the long board.

All parts are cut and ready to assemble.

1. Begin with the front and back, cutting both ends of the piece to 90° peaks, and then separating them at the correct lengths—5¾" each from roof peak to base.

2. Cut the ½" clips on one end of the 3½"-wide piece.

3. Separate that piece into the 3½"-tall sides and the 3½"-square (minus clips) floor.

4. Drill the ⅞"-entry hole at eave level in the front piece.

5. Place the sides upright and spaced the width of the front apart. Place glue on one side's edge and align front and drive two or three 1" brads to hold it in place as the glue dries.

6. Repeat the process with the second side.

7. Turn the assembled sides and front upside down, place glue on the side edges now up, and glue and nail the back in place.

8. Install the short side of the roof, using glue and brads to hold it in place. The overhang is adjustable, though it needs to be even for both parts of the roof. The top edge of this short side should just touch each of the eave peaks.

9. The longer roof side goes on now. Place a bead of glue on each eave part and along the edge of the shorter piece of roof already in place. Place the roof piece so it is even with the top edge of the shorter piece and use brads to hold it in place.

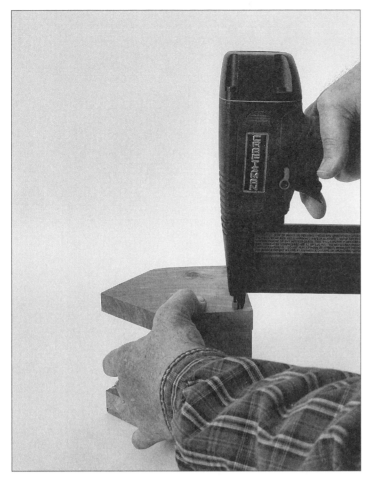

Use brads and glue to assemble sides to front and back.

Check fit of walnut trim pieces. These short pieces were cut on a hand miter box.

Glue the walnut strips in place after assembling all but the floor of the wren house.

10. Finish clipping the floor so it will drain well. One note here for those who don't wish to get this close to a spinning blade: you can readily trim these edges with almost any power sander, especially with soft-woods such as red cedar and pine. We used a 12" Delta disc sander, but that much size, while very handy, is not essential. The clips may also be made in a hand miter box, or even with a band saw or scroll saw.

11. Cut the trim pieces to size. We elected to miter the pieces, but it's not necessary. Use a hand miter box for these. The little Jorgenson maple miter box added to a Freud Gent's saw works like a charm for this kind of work.

12. Glue the trim in place. Top-edge gluing needs a long-reach clamp to get around the roof (or you can glue it in place before installing the roof). The spring clamps shown worked beautifully for the bottom pieces.

13. Install the floor, drilling pilot holes through the sides and into the floor, and then run in #6 x 1½" washer head screws.

Aerial view of finished wren house.

PROJECT FIVE
ROBIN NESTING SHELF

Robins nest fairly high, and don't nest in enclosed "houses" or sites. They do love to nest on ledges, though, so it makes sense to build the robins in your yard their own ledges, which you can then install up under an outbuilding's eaves.

The shelf is more easily made from exterior-grade plywood, because of the quality of most pine in lumberyards today. We had picked up some pine at a local big box store and tried to work around the splits, cups, and warps (after selecting the best boards on hand out of about 45). Given time to do another, we'd go for ¾" B-B or B-C exterior plywood. Or we'd pay the 125% premium for "premium" wood, which wasn't all that great either.

Materials:
1 piece ¾" x 8" x 16¼" pine or plywood for backboard
1 piece ¾" x 8¼" x 10" pine or plywood for one roof side
1 piece ¾" x 3⅞" x 10" pine or plywood for second roof side
1 piece ¾" x 8" x 6" pine or plywood for arched side
1 piece ¾" x 8" x 10" pine or plywood for floor
1 piece ¾" x ¾" x 19" cedar molding (made at the same time as the logs were made for the later log cabin birdhouse)
paint

Robin Nesting Shelf Side Pattern

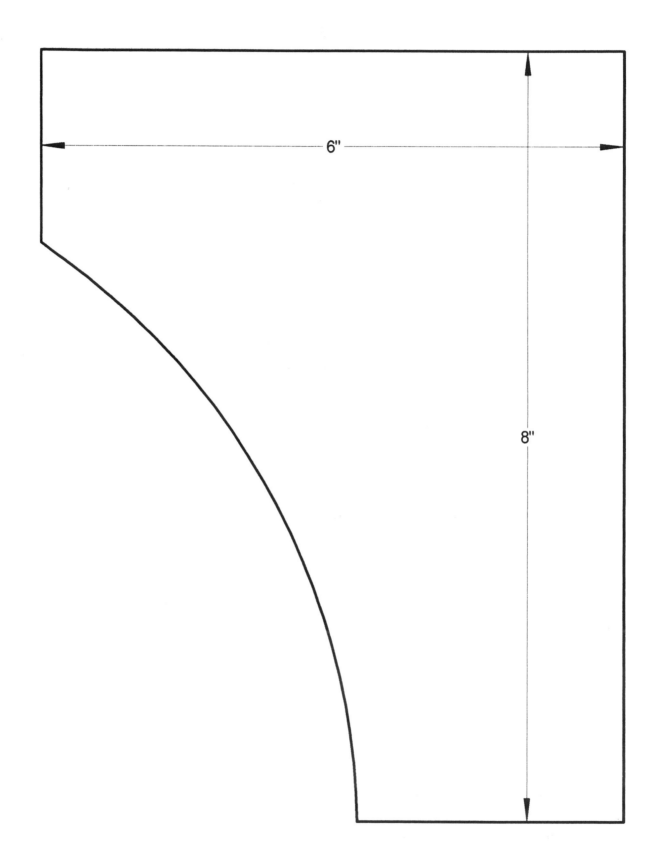

6"

8"

Robin Nesting Shelf

Cut backboard from ¾" stock. Cut one roof piece 10" deep by 8¼" wide. Cut other piece 3⅞" wide by 10". Cut edge board for left side 8" tall by 8" deep and bevel top at 45 degrees.

Cut base 8" wide by 10" deep.

Backboard is 16¼" tall by 8" wide.

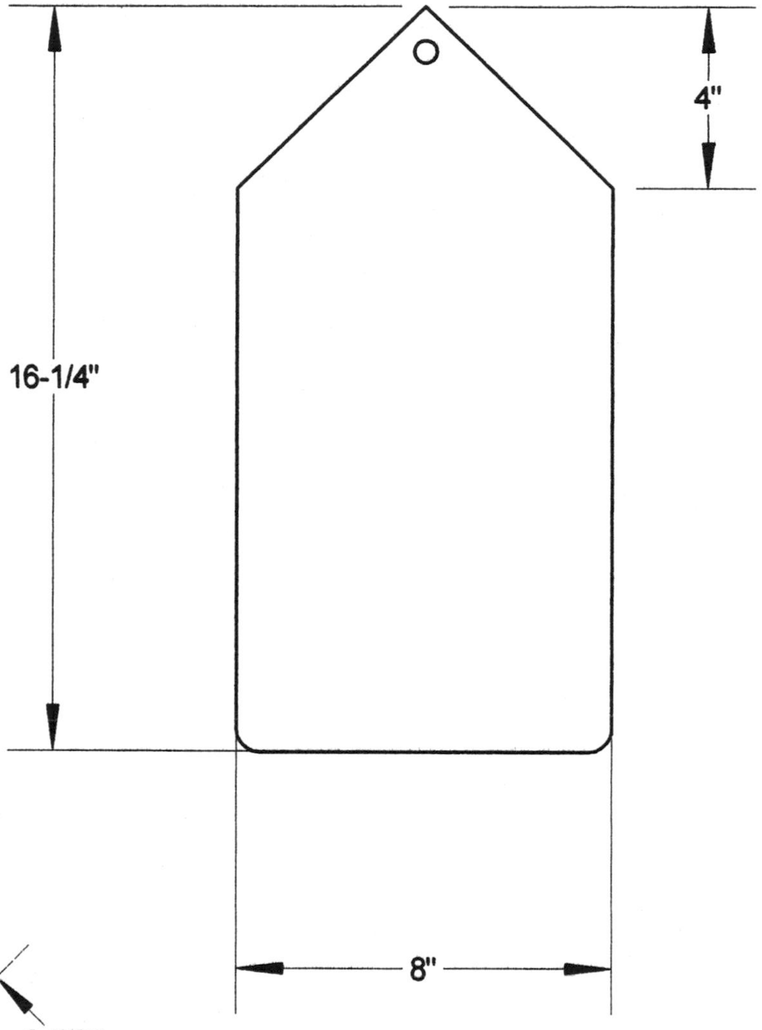

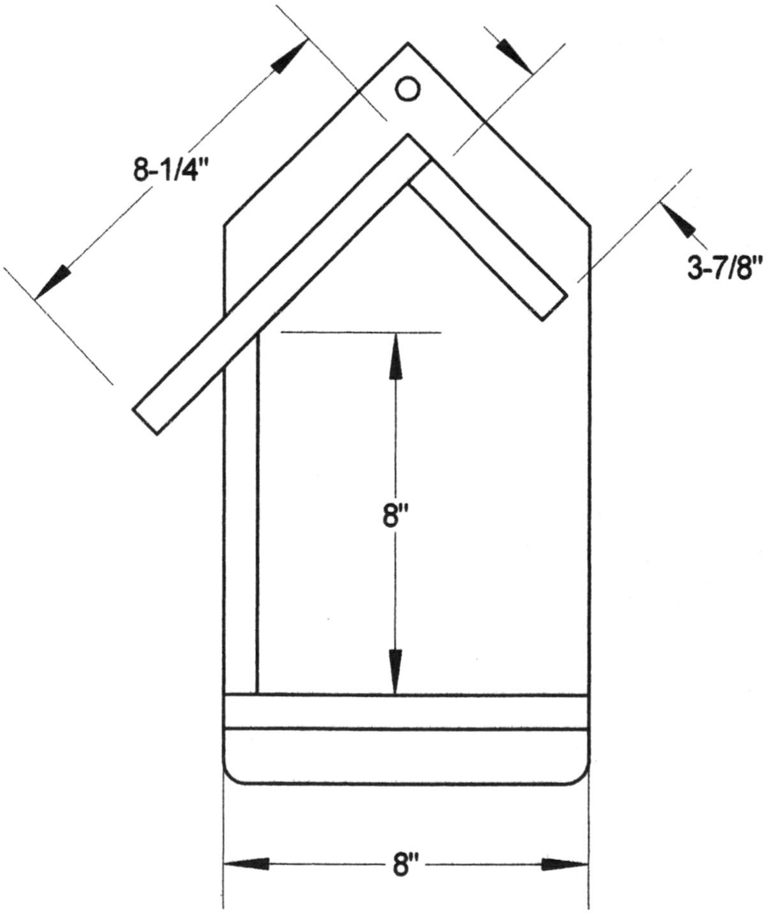

16-1/4"

4"

8"

8-1/4"

3-7/8"

8"

8"

Bottom curves on back are marked with 6" random orbit sander discs.

1. Start by cutting the backboard to length, and then cutting the 90° angle at the top (two 45° miters).

2. Cut the bottom curves to about a 1" on the backboard.

3. Cut the shelf to size, 8" x 10".

4. Cut the side to size and bevel its top edge to 45°.

5. Tape the full-sized pattern onto the side and cut that out.

6. Cut the floor to its final 8" x 10" size.

7. Mark front and back for the floor position, place glue on the edge and along the backboard, and drive 1¼" or 1½" brads into the rear floor edge from the backboard. Keep your fingers well away from the exit points for the brads if you're using a pneumatic brad nailer.

8. Place the arched side with its flat side along the backboard and its bottom on the floor. The 45° bevel faces the outside of the platform. Use glue and 1" brads to fasten the side in place.

9. Assemble the roof, with the short side as shown in the drawing. Use glue and brads to hold it together.

For curved parts, use a band saw or scroll saw to follow the lines.

Use brads to assemble the roof after the glue is applied to both sides.

Check roof fit.

Glue side in place.

Sand all edges.

Checking shelf rail placement.

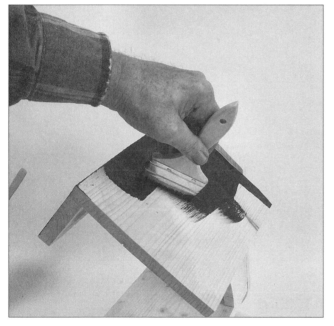

Painting the roof.

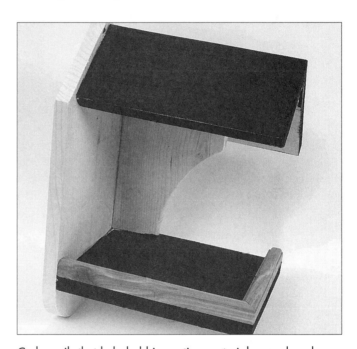

Cedar rails that help hold in nesting materials are placed.

10. Place the roof, marking the rear of the backboard. The simplest method is to apply glue, clamp the roof in place, then measure the front and transfer the measurements. The short side of the roof comes to about within ¾" of the right edge. Once the marks are made, use them to drive 1¼" brads into the roof from the rear of the backboard.

11. Remove the clamps and paint the roof, and other parts, as desired. We used a brush-on **Red Devil** enamel.

12. Once the paint has dried, cut 45° angles in the end of each molding piece, and install with glue and 1" brads. Scrape the paint from the area underneath the molding so the glue can grip.

13. Hang from screws at the top and bottom.

PROJECT SIX
COLONIAL SALTBOX
for Titmice and Nuthatches

This saltbox design used up the last of the redwood we had around here from back in our deck-building days. Changing the entry hole to 1⅜" makes it suitable for nuthatches.

Materials:
1 piece ¾" x 5½" x 5⅜" redwood or red cedar for front
1 piece ¾" x 5½" x 3⅜" redwood or red cedar for back
2 pieces ¾" x 7" x 7⅜" redwood or cedar for sides
1 piece ¾" x 10" x 8" redwood or red cedar for base
1 piece ¾" x 8" x 8" redwood or red cedar for back roof
1 piece ¾" x 8" x 3⅜" redwood or red cedar for front roof
1 piece ¾" x 8" x 3⅛" redwood or red cedar for porch roof
1 piece 1½"D pipe floor flange
1 piece 1½"D x 10' galvanized pipe, one end threaded to fit pipe flange
brads
screws
Titebond III
cold set epoxy

Colonial Saltbox

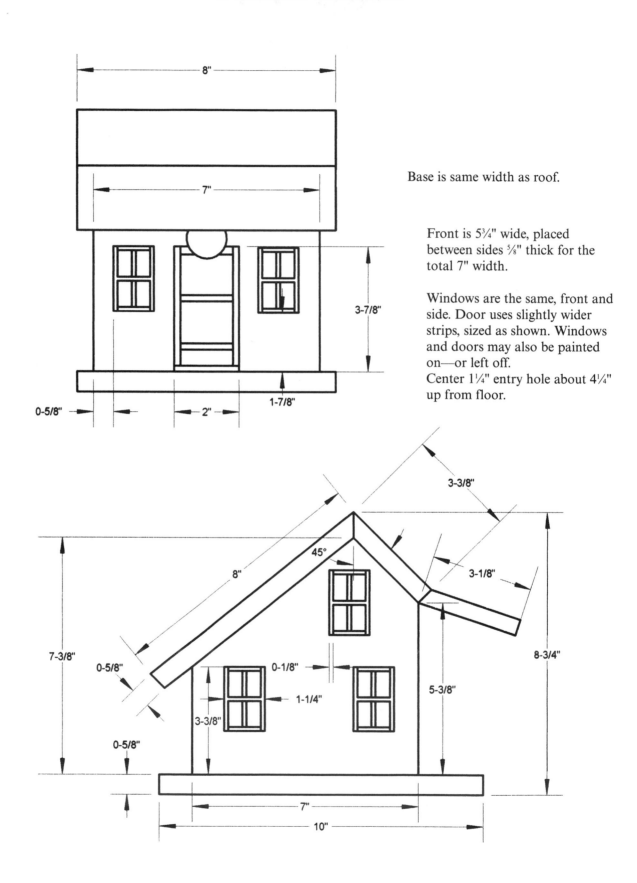

Base is same width as roof.

Front is 5¾" wide, placed between sides ⅝" thick for the total 7" width.

Windows are the same, front and side. Door uses slightly wider strips, sized as shown. Windows and doors may also be painted on—or left off.
Center 1¼" entry hole about 4¼" up from floor.

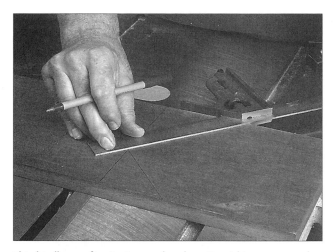

This birdhouse fits titmice, nuthatches, Bewick's wrens, and a few other birds, with a 1¼" entry hole. Here, the rear roof line is laid out on the side of the house.

Rip the redwood to size.

Use a light-colored backerboard with redwood.

Drill the entry hole with a hand drill and Forstner bit.

1. Cut the sides to size. Tape them together tightly.

2. Set the miter saw so it starts 3⅜" at the rear of the sides, and rises to 8¾".

3. Set the saw so that it cuts from 5⅜" to 8¾" up for the front roof angle. Remove tape when cuts are finished.

4. Cut the rear wall to 3⅜" tall and 5½" wide.

5. Cut the front wall to 5⅜" tall and 5½" wide.

6. Drill the 1¼"-entry hole about 4" up on the front wall, centered from edge to edge.

7. Use clamps and glue to assemble front and back to one side. Brad nail to allow removal of clamps, or wait at least two hours for the glue to set.

8. Once glue has set, place end wall down, with front and back extending up, and glue and nail the second end in place.

9. Bevel top edges of roof at 45°, for both front and rear pieces.

The light-colored chips show when you've broken through, while the tightly held backboard keeps the back of the hole from splintering.

Check fit of all bevels and miters before gluing. Where the fit isn't good, sand or plane.

10. Assemble that section of the roof using Titebond III and a couple of brads. Use corner clamps to support the assembly.

11. Bevel the porch roof back edge to 25°, using a table saw or a plane. This piece is too narrow and too long to be safely beveled on a compound miter saw. With a table saw, make and use a zero clearance insert, and keep the guard in place.

12. Assemble porch roof to regular roof using epoxy. There is no other really secure way to fasten this angle.

13. Center pipe flange on base and screw it in place with galvanized or brass wood screws.

14. Use four washer head #6 x 1¼" screws to fasten the base onto the house itself.

15. If you desire, draw on the windows and door before installing the roof. You may also buy dollhouse windows and doors and place them with glue. Sand the birdhouse before installing the windows and doors, and before drawing them on.

16. Install the roof. Run a line of glue down each eave on the house, and measure and mark both sides of the roof, putting a line of glue down each underside. Lay the roof in place and fasten with 1¼" brads.

17. Sand lightly and spray with clear finish.

18. Install the post in a dug hole, and tamp down well.

19. Install the finished birdhouse on the post by turning it onto the male post threads.

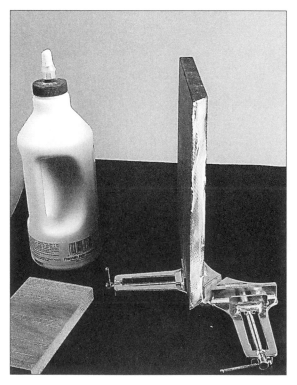

Corner clamps are a great help when edge gluing bevels.

Here, you see the assembled birdhouse body. I used a magic marker to outline the windows and door. You may use dollhouse doors and windows or just ignore them.

Use a plumbing floor flange for the size pipe you will use as a post. Here, the diameter is 1½".

The base is screwed onto the bottom of the house, so it can be removed for clean-out when the breeding season is over.

Top view of colonial saltbox.

PROJECT SEVEN
DOWNY WOODPECKER HOUSE

This is another simple-to-build house, made from cypress, so it doesn't need a finish, though is not hurt by one, either. Cypress is an easy-to-work wood, and is generally only available at wood dealers, so the quality tends to be quite high compared to pines. Red cedar also works well for this birdhouse.

Materials:
1 piece ¾" x 24" x 5½" red cedar or cypress for back and front
2 pieces ¾" x 4" x 6" red cedar or cypress for sides
1 piece ¾" x 4" x 4" red cedar or cypress for bottom
1 piece ¾" x 5¼" x 7" red cedar or cypress for one roof piece
1 piece ¾" x 6" x 7" red cedar or cypress for second roof piece
Titebond III wood glue
brads

Downy Woodpecker House

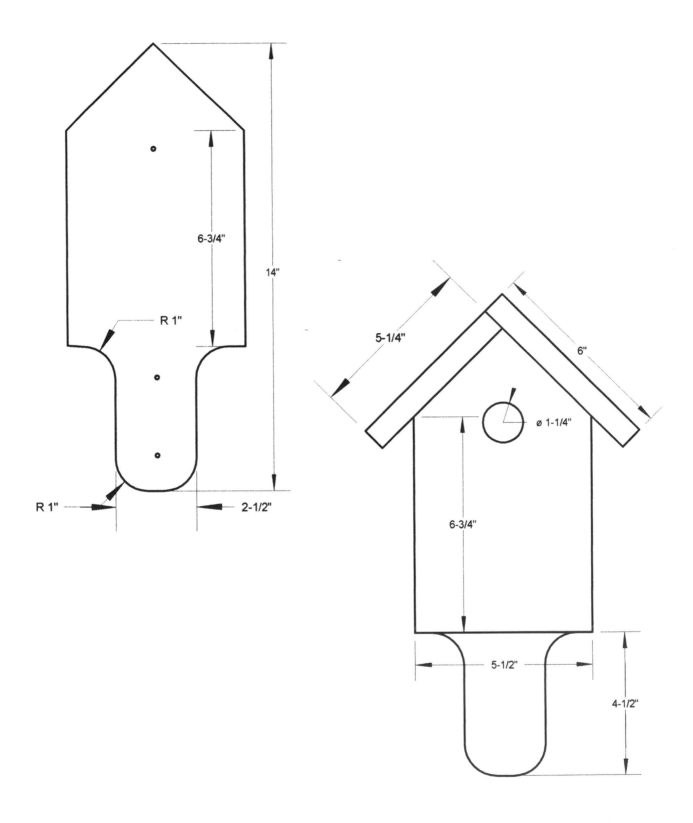

6-3/4"

14"

R 1"

R 1"

2-1/2"

5-1/4"

6"

ø 1-1/4"

6-3/4"

5-1/2"

4-1/2"

Downy Woodpecker House

Sides are 6" tall x 4" wide.
One roof section is 5¼" high by 7" long.
The second roof piece is 6" tall by 7" long.

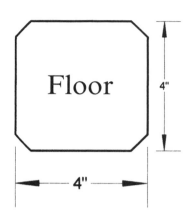

Floor

4"

4"

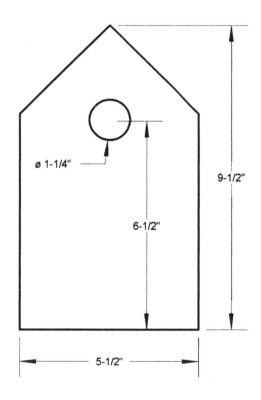

ø 1-1/4"

9-1/2"

6-1/2"

5-1/2"

Parts for the downy woodpecker house.

The cypress front is added to the sides.

1. Rip back and front to width, 5½".
2. Cut each end to 45° from both sides—the result is a 90° peak at each end.
3. Separate the 9½"-long front.
4. Trim the back to 14".
5. Drill the 1¼"-hole with its center point at 6¾" up the front.
6. Mark the bottom of the back 2½" wide on center, and then mark that with 1" radius curves at top and bottom edges: the top edges are set 4½" up from the bottom.
7. Cut the curves with a band saw or a jigsaw, or a scroll saw.
8. Assemble the 6"-tall sides to the front, using brads and glue.
9. Assemble the back to the sides, using brads and glue and setting the sides even with the top edge of the peak on the back (so that the front peak and the rear peak are even).

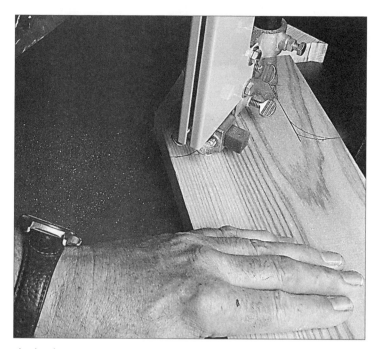

The back section curves are cut on a band saw here, but a scroll saw works, too.

Use washer head screws to make the base removable.

10. Place the short side of the roof on the peak, even with the peak edges. Glue and nail in place.

11. Place the long side of the roof even with the edge of the short side and glue and nail in place.

12. Use three #6 x 1¼" washer head screws to fasten the floor in place. Removing those screws allows for easy clean-out at the end of the nesting season.

13. Sand as needed.

14. You may leave unfinished or spray on a clear exterior polyurethane finish. We sprayed this one with a clear ZAR exterior poly, using a Critter spray gun. The clear finish retards the cypress's turning gray in the weather.

The completed house is ready to install.

PROJECT EIGHT
LOG CABIN
Using Square Cedar Logs with Rounded Outside Log Edges

This project attracts attention because of the colorful red cedar logs. The eave ends may also be painted a bright color, though we didn't do that here. It is easier to make than it looks, but is quite time-consuming because each log must be glued and each brad nailed in place.

Making the logs is simplicity itself. Use a wider cedar board to form the edges of the logs, running them across a very small roundover bit on a router table—the router table doesn't have to be fancy. The one you see here is a Vermont-American model similar to one carried by Sears, Roebuck under the Craftsman name, and it's easy to use.

Once the edges are curved on two sides of the board, simply run the board through the tablesaw and cut the edges off. Repeat as needed, depending on board length. Then cut to length, and there you are.

For the roof, we used scrap exotics floating around. Four of the boards were mahogany, but the darker peak boards were unknown, very heavy wood. We also did one of the versions with walnut boards (walnut is a reasonably durable wood), but the boards were too thick and didn't work as well, as far as appearance is concerned.

Materials:

1 piece ¾" x 12" x 8" pine for eave ends
1 piece ¾" x 6½" x 6½" red cedar or cypress for floor
4 pieces ⅜" x 10" x 4" red cedar or other boards for roof
2 pieces ⅜" x 10" x 2½" red cedar or other boards for roof peak
glue
brads

Log Cabin

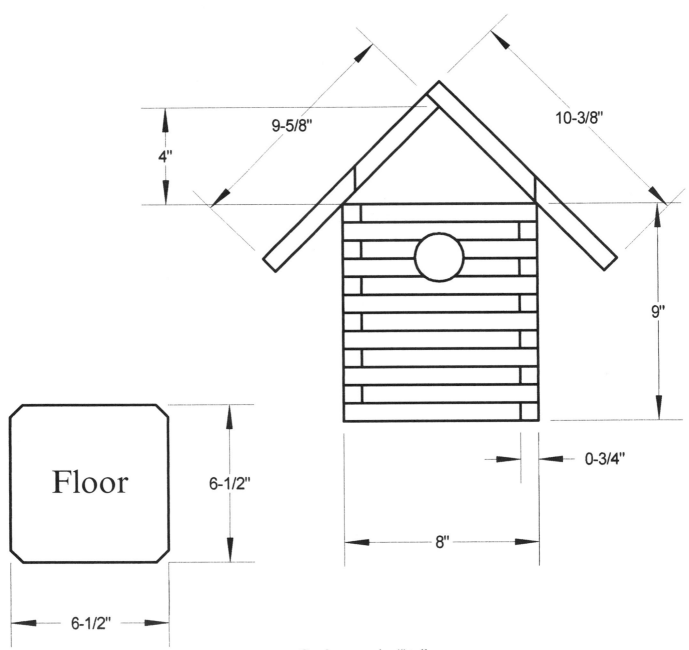

9-5/8"

4"

10-3/8"

9"

0-3/4"

Floor

6-1/2"

6-1/2"

8"

Cut 2 eave ends, 4" tall.

Cut 48 logs 7¼" long.

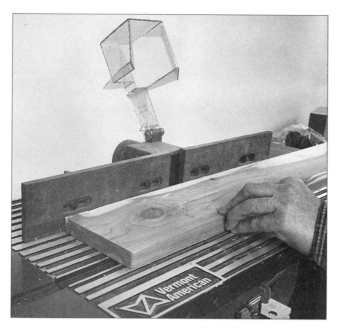

Using a router table to start rounding log edges.

Rounding the second edge of a log.

Roundover is very slight.

Starting assembly of log stack.

1. Select the pine for the eave ends and mark up the center on both sides.

2. Make the four 45° cuts that form the peaks, using both ends of the board.

3. Cut one board to length, right at the base of the peak, and then do the other.

4. Start making cedar logs by setting up the router with a small roundover bit.

5. Feed a 4" or wider red cedar board through the router table, doing both edges of both sides. Round over as many edges as you need to make your logs, plus an allowance for mistakes (two logs should be enough; most log cabins use about 48 logs, some use fewer).

6. Set the table saw to rip ¾" wide and rip off the rounded-over sections.

Adding more logs.

Finished log stack. It's time to wipe off excess glue.

Entry hole drilled and first eave end added.

Both eave ends in place.

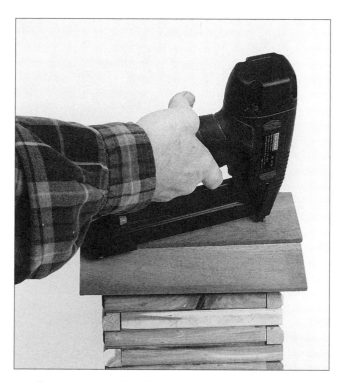

Installing exotic wood roof.

Finished cabin, walnut roof.

7. Use a miter saw to cut the logs to 8" lengths.

8. As you see in the photos, lay out the first-row logs. As the stack rises, you alternate the log ends. Each log is placed on the one under with Titebond III wood glue and two 1" brads. Use a square on the flat insides of the walls to keep the logs straight as they go up. A little crookedness makes these log cabins look more rustic, though.

9. When the logs have reached their required height, let the glue dry for about half an hour to an hour. Mark and drill the entry hole after that. Use a Forstner bit. Ours is drilled for bluebirds, but you may also drill this house for flycatchers or white-breasted nuthatches (1½").

10. Once the hole is drilled, attach the eave ends. Use glue and 1¼" nails down through the edges about 1" or 1½" end from the slender ends of the eave triangles.

11. Allow at least a 1" overhang in front and glue and nail the roof boards in place.

12. The floor goes in with two or three washer head #6 x 1¼" screws so it can be readily removed for cleaning the house at season's end.

PROJECT NINE
DECAGONAL BIRDHOUSE
for Bluebirds

The body of this house is made of strips of white oak, while the roof and floor are made from pine. The lift at the front of the roof is of osage orange, but that's because there was some scrap around the shop. Use whatever wood you have on hand.

This is a little more complex than most of the birdhouses, but is not truly difficult if you have a tablesaw capable of making accurate 18° bevels on the strips of oak.

Do not cut the roof or base or elevation materials until after you have assembled the barrel for the house. Variations are easily possible, depending on the actual thickness of your wood and the accuracy of your saw.

Materials:
2 pieces ¾" x 3" x 72" white oak for side staves
2 pieces ¾" x 7⅛" x 7⅛" pine, cedar, or cypress for roof and base
1 piece ¾" x 6⅛" x 3" strip of wood for roof elevation at front
glue
brads
#6 x 1¼" washer head wood screws

Decagonal Bluebird House

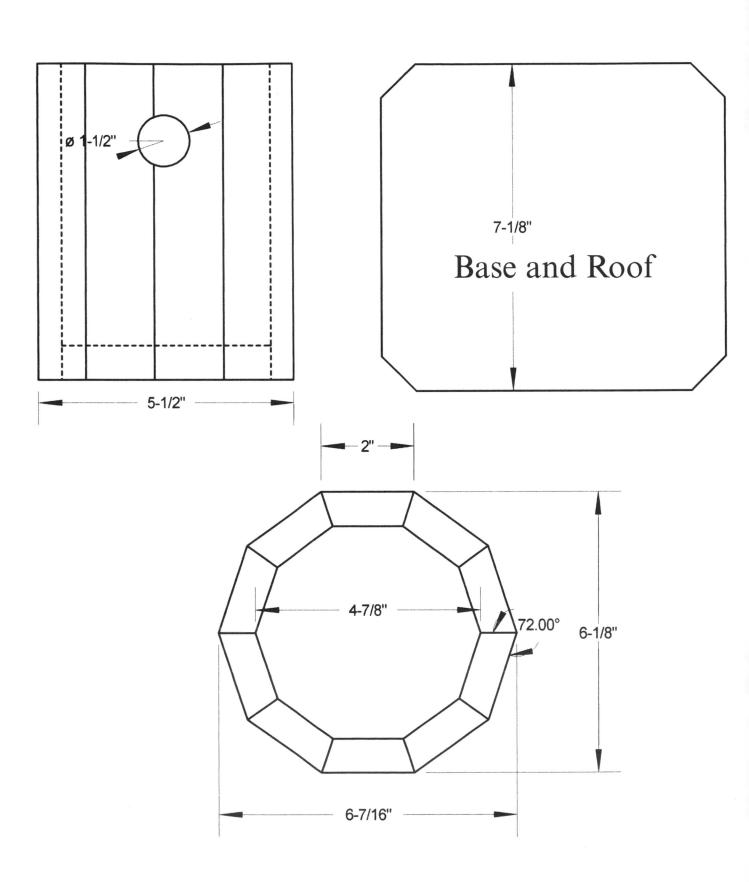

ø 1-1/2"

5-1/2"

7-1/8"

Base and Roof

2"

4-7/8"

72.00°

6-1/8"

6-7/16"

Always use a push stick when working close to the blade, even with the guard.

Keep mark to right of the blade when the cut-off piece is also on the right.

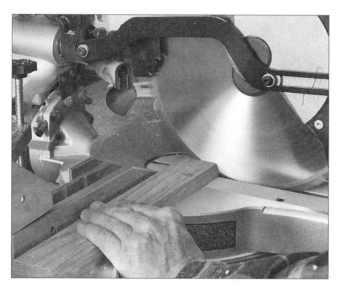

Make cuts slowly with a power miter saw because just chopping down tears the wood a lot, even with a top-quality blade.

Use the first cut-off piece to mark the remaining cuts, one at a time.

1. Start by selecting good white oak. If you wish to paint the whole birdhouse, use any wood, but white oak is durable. Pieces need to be wide enough to allow good ripping at a bevel. We set the saw for a 2" width.

2. You are working close to the blade here, so a good push stick is an essential. Feed the oak at a reasonable speed and cut one side, and then the next, without changing the blade set up, if possible.

3. Use the compound miter saw to cut oak to length. Each piece is 6¾" long. Use the first piece to measure each of the next nine pieces.

4. Lay two strips of 1½" or wider masking tape on a clean surface, sticky side up.

5. Place the first piece, narrow side up, carefully square to the strips.

6. Place the remaining piece butted carefully on the first piece, and then on each succeeding piece so that there are no gaps.

7. Roll the 10 strips up to check the fit. If adjustment is needed, remove the offending piece and use a very sharp block plane to trim.

8. With the tape package unrolled again, apply glue to both sides of every piece.

Lay out two strips of masking tape, adhesive side up.

Align cut sides on the two pieces of tape.

Roll most of the way up without glue to check the fit.

Apply glue.

Roll up on the tape.

Most of the glue squeeze-out is on the inside.

Put on a band clamp just tight enough to give glue squeeze-out. The masking tape can't supply quite enough pressure.

The step up is marked and cut and then installed with screws. Drill pilot holes. I used a piece of scrap osage orange.

9. Carefully roll the package up.

10. Place a band clamp around the center, or close to it, of the roll. In the photos, you see a Jorgenson Pony band clamp. It is handy, easy to use and reasonably low cost. The strap is wide enough to do the job well. Tighten firmly but not super tight. You want to barely create more glue squeeze-out.

11. Wipe off all the squeeze-out you can reach.

12. After at least six hours, you can release the clamp, peel off the tape, and continue.

13. Nail and glue the riser to the front edge of the roof.

14. Drill the hole for the birds you wish to attract. The 1½"-hole is useful for several.

15. Install the base with brads and glue into the base.

16. Install the roof with the #6 x 1¼" washer head screws.

17. This decagonal birdhouse is designed to mount on top of a fence or other post, with the removable roof off and a screw or two driven down through the base into the post. The roof serves as access for cleaning the house out.

Project Ten
Chickadee House with Concave Roof
(with a smaller version for a wren)

Chickadees are friendly little birds that light on your finger when you hold a hand out with some sunflower seeds—and a bit of patience, as it takes 10 or 15 minutes.

Encouraging them to hang around and to reproduce is a great idea, so this small bird-house is designed to help at that point.

Any wood may be used, but this version is of cypress, and the roof slats are purpleheart. As noted elsewhere, we had a good bit of scrap or near-scrap purpleheart from years gone by.

Materials:
1 piece ¾" x 21" x 5½" cypress for front and back
1 piece ¾" x 12" x 5" cypress for sides
1 piece ¾" x 4" x 4½" cypress for floor
12 roof slats about ¼" x 2" x 7½" purpleheart or other durable wood
brads
Titebond III glue
2 #6 x 1¼" washer head screws

Chickadee House with Concave Roof

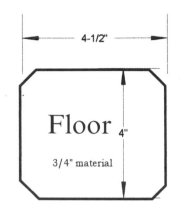

Floor

4-1/2"

4"

3/4" material

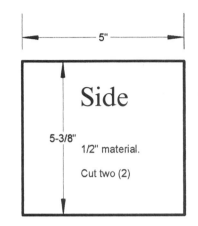

Side

5"

5-3/8"

1/2" material.

Cut two (2)

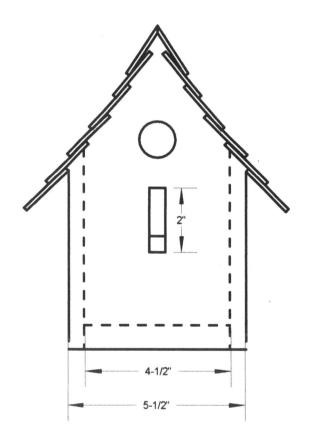

2"

4-1/2"

5-1/2"

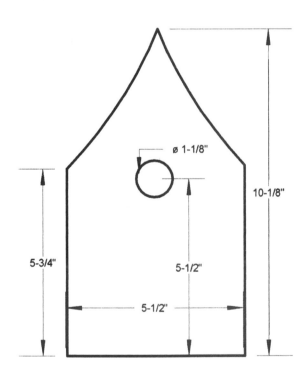

ø 1-1/8"

10-1/8"

5-3/4"

5-1/2"

5-1/2"

Chickadee House with Concave Roof

Full-size eave outline
Mark, or tape, on 10⅛" tall front and back.

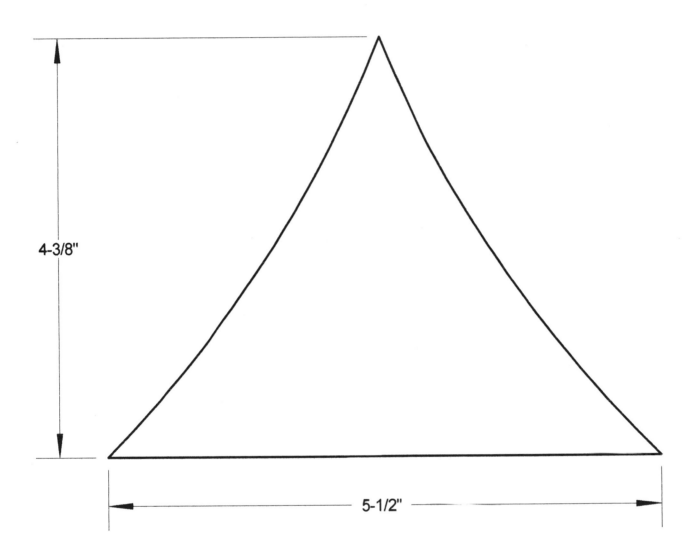

4-3/8"

5-1/2"

Cutting roof eave arcs.

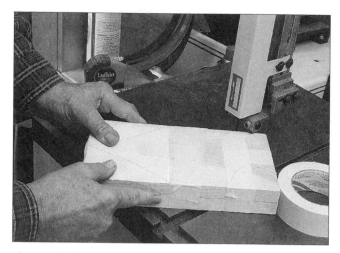

Placing the full-sized paper pattern, with masking tape.

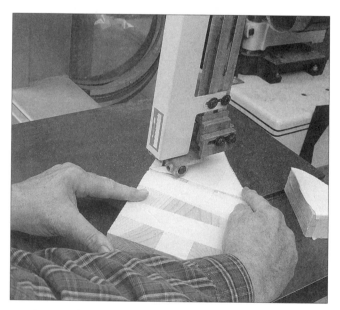

Finishing roof eave arc cuts.

The eave curve is modest, easy to cut.

1. Begin by ripping the cypress to 5½" wide for the front and back.

2. Cut the cypress, square on both ends, to 10⅛" tall and tape the two pieces tightly together.

3. Next, tape the full-sized pattern on the cypress.

4. Use a band saw, jigsaw, or scroll saw to follow the curved pattern taped on the cypress.

5. Cut the sides to size, first ripping to 5" wide, and then cutting to 5⅜" length.

6. Cut the floor to 4" x 4½", and clip the corners ½" each for drainage.

7. Cut roofing material as needed for thickness and then cut to 7½" lengths.

8. Drill the 1⅛"-entry hole with the center at about the point where the lower edges of the eaves fall.

9. Place the front on the two sides (5" side vertical) to check alignment and fit. Remove the front.

10. Coat one side's edge with glue and carefully align that side and the front, using the unglued side to support the front.

Drilling the entry hole.

The finished chickadee-sized hole.

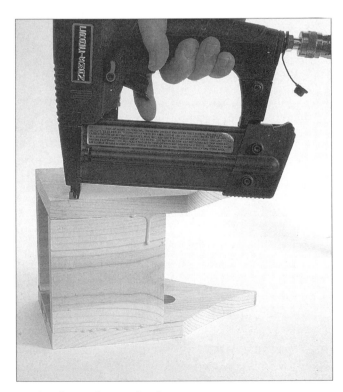

Use brads to substitute for clamping.

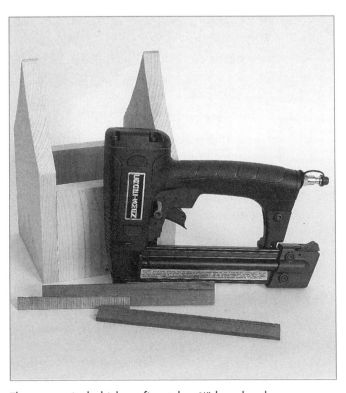

The quarter-inch-thick roofing takes ⅜"-long brads.

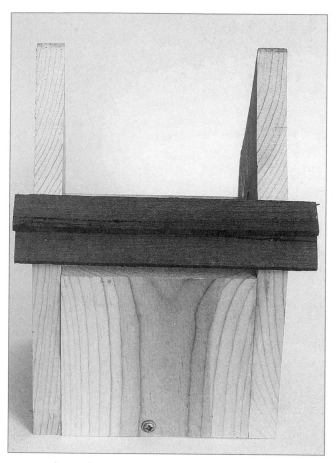

Starting the roofing is simple, and done from the bottom. Keep overlap as even as possible going up.

A shorter version, with a slightly extended roof arc, is set up as a wren house and uses a purpleheart rectangle as an entry aid.

11. Use three brads to fasten the first side in place.

12. Repeat the glue and brad placement with the second side.

13. Turn the front facedown so the fastened sides are vertical and place the back on those sides, checking alignment and making any needed corrections.

14. Place glue on the edges of both sides, replace the back, and use three brad nails on each side to fasten it while the glue dries.

15. Install the floor, using pilot holes before inserting the #6 x 1¼" screws.

16. Stand the birdhouse on its base, and start installing the roofing boards. Leave about ⅜" overlap after the first board (which should bet about a 1" overhang). Mark for each board if you wish to be really careful, and use a single ⅝"-long brad and glue as you rise up the roof.

17. The top edge of the roof may be sealed with silicone seal or epoxy.

18. If you wish, use a 3" x ½" x ⅜" piece of purpleheart to form a perch under the entry hole.

A modified version of the birdhouse described in this section, intended for wrens, is pictured above. Everything is pretty much the same, except the birdhouse is made out of painted redwood, has a beveled side, and is only 8½" tall, total. Use the same pattern to form the eaves, but extend them out, since this house is 6¼" wide instead of 5½". This means ⅜" on each side needs to be extended for the pattern to work. The edge of the lower wall will be 3½" tall if all works. The bevel is not necessary but makes for a nicer look. Side length is 5", set inside the front and back, and the floor is 4½" x 5", placed with washer head screws.

PROJECT ELEVEN
PURPLE MARTIN HOUSE

Purple martins are bug-eaters supreme and are also sociable birds—with other purple martins. Many birds don't like to live in colonies. Martins do. Because they are so hard on insect life, that gives us a benefit.

Purple martin houses must be placed high, usually on a sectioned pole that can be lowered so the nests can be cleaned during the off-season. You could end up feeling a bit like an innkeeper, but it's worth it.

The birdhouse is a mix of sassafras—a durable and great-smelling wood—cypress, and a pine roof and floors. The pine needs painting, or soon will.

This birdhouse takes more material than any other, and is designed in sections so that they can be stacked. You can easily add two or four more apartments to this unit just by building more bottom units. By doubling the width, you can make double the spaces on each floor, but that also takes one more divider (but doesn't need a back wall).

Materials:

1 piece ¾" x 7½" x 20" cypress for eave ends

1 piece ¾" x 6" x 24" cypress or sassafras for dividers

4 pieces ¾" x 14" x 6" sassafras for sides and front

1 piece ¾" x 7½" x 6" cypress for first-story ends

2 pieces ¾" x 9½" x 15½" pine for platforms (Exterior plywood is a better choice)

1 piece ¾" x 5¾" x 17" pine for roof

1 piece ¾" x 6½" x 17" pine for roof

4 galvanized 1½" hook and eye sets

brads

Titebond III wood glue

101

Purple Martin House

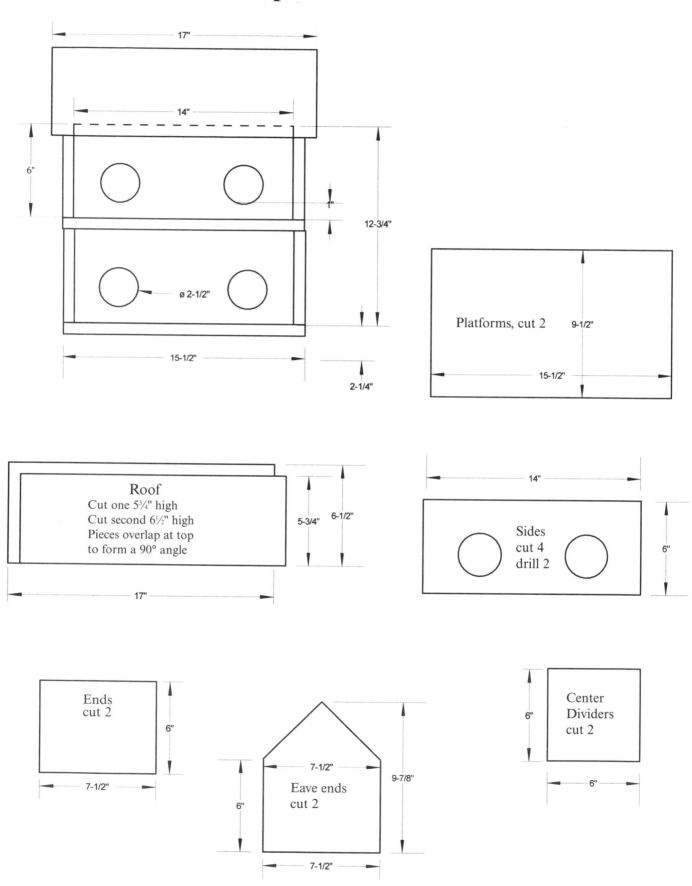

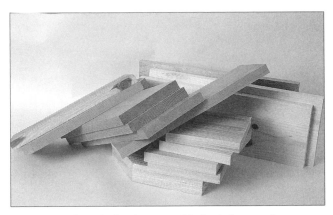

Parts cut and ready for the start of hole drilling and assembly.

Cleanly cut chips of this size indicate a very sharp bit.

Glue and nail cypress ends to sassafras front and back.

Nail and glue on first side of roof.

1. Cut the eave ends. Set the compound miter saw to 45°, and mark the board up the middle on both sides. Cut and flip, reverse ends and cut and flip, using the center mark as the tall edge of the eave.

2. Cut each eave end to 9⅞" tall.

3. Rip all four sides to 6" wide, and cut to 14" long.

4. Drill 2½"-diameter entry holes high enough to leave at least a 1¼" lip below them.

5. Cut two center divers to 6" squares.

6. Cut two first-story ends, 6" x 7½", from cypress.

7. Rip one roof section 5¾" wide and make it 17" long.

8. Rip the second roof section to 6½" wide and cut to the same 17" length.

9. Cut two platforms 9½" wide x 15½" long. These are installed with ends flush with the martin house ends, and with a lip, or porch, for the birds in front.

10. Assemble the box for the first floor using either silicon bronze wood screws or nails and glue. This time, it works best if you can hold the front in something like a Black & Decker Workmate to make it easy to place and nail the ends. Glue first, then nail.

Finish up by nailing and gluing second side of roof in place.

The top floor is assembled, with sides placed inside the ends.

The top floor was assembled with silicone bronze screws that were countersunk.

Remove rough spots around holes (I didn't use a tight enough backer-board here) with a rotary tool, but make sure it is turned down. At its top speed, it skids the sanding drum all over the wood.

Hooks and eyes hold the upper and lower sections together, and allow easy cleaning of the bottom section, plus easy stacking of extra stories if desired. Use an awl or thin-bladed screwdriver to turn the hooks and eyes in. It's much easier on the fingers.

All sections are assembled and ready for finish.

11. Place the divider in the center of the bottom unit, again gluing and nailing in place.

12. Assemble the upper story in the same manner, using the Workmate or a similar holding tool to prevent misalignment. This time, we used the silicon bronze screws to hold things together.

13. Add the narrow roof section to the upper story eaves, placing glue on the eaves and brad nailing the piece so that its top edge is even with the peak of eaves. Overhang is ¼" of an inch at each end. You can simplify setting by just tack nailing a ¼"-wide piece at one edge. That lines it up on both sides. Pull the piece off once the section is nailed in place.

14. Add the wider section of the roof, lining it up with the upper edge of the narrow section. No markers should be needed. Place glue on the eave edges and along the upper edge of the narrow roof piece, and nail just enough to hold in place while the glue dries.

15. The platform for the upper story goes on with four flat head screws, after you place the divider with glue and nails.

16. The edges are even, so countersink the screws ⅜" inch in from that board's edge, and screw in place without glue. This allows clean-out later.

17. The bottom platform is nailed and glued in place, because lifting off the top section gives access for cleaning. Paint the platform before installing it, and give the paint plenty of time to dry. All the overhang is to the front.

18. Install the hooks and eyes at each end, as you see in the photos. Pilot holes are a big help in making installation easy, but using a small shanked screwdriver or an awl to do the turning is an even bigger help. Getting this reasonably tight is important, as this does all the work of holding the top section in place. If you decide to add extra stories to the house, go up to 2" hook-and-eye sets.

You may wish to paint the roof, or you may want to add some other roofing. We haven't decided yet, so it is unfinished in the photographs.

PROJECT TWELVE
FLYCATCHER HOUSE

The flycatcher house is in some ways our fanciest design, but in every way is very simple to build. The roof is another overlay style, and the fence was bought at a local craft store, where you can usually find four or five patterns and sizes. You may also make your own fence, if you're so inclined.

Materials:

4 fence sections from craft store
1 piece ¾" x 23¼" x 7" pine for front and back
1 piece ¾" x 11" x 9½" pine for base
1 piece ¾" x 5" x 16" white oak for sides (7¾"-tall each)
1 piece ¾" x 5½" x 5" pine for floor
1 piece ¾" x 7¾" x 8" pine for wide roof section
1 piece ¾" x 7" x 8" pine for narrow roof section
6 pieces ¼"D x 2" dowel for fence posts
white paint
blue paint
red paint

Flycatcher House

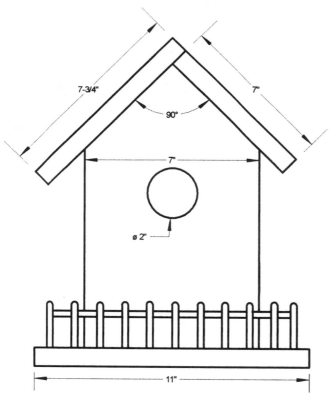

Sides are 7¾" tall by 5" wide. This height leaves ventilation space. Use ¾" wood.

One roof part is 7" long (or tall) and the second is 7¾". Use ¾"-thick wood and make the tops 8" wide (1" overhang, front and rear).

The base and floor may be screwed or epoxied together. Clip the floor edges, as in other plans, and then drill down, using a ⅜" bit, at each corner after the floor is attached to the base. The entire unit is held in place with 3 washer head screws.

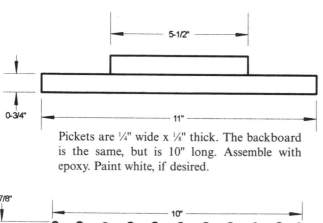

Pickets are ¼" wide x ⅛" thick. The backboard is the same, but is 10" long. Assemble with epoxy. Paint white, if desired.

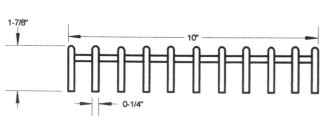

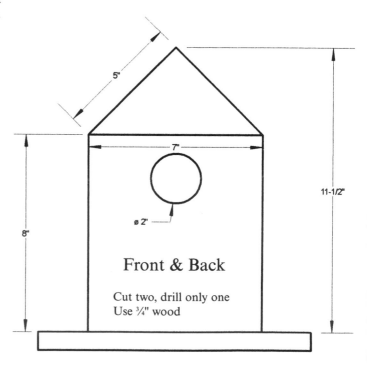

Front & Back

Cut two, drill only one
Use ¾" wood

My hand looks closer than it is. Always keep hands well clear of spinning blades.

The wood was badly cupped, so the saw snatched a piece. Never fight such an action. This is why you wear safety glasses, too.

1. Rip the pine to 7" width for the front and back, squaring the ends so it is 23¼" long.

2. Separate those pieces using the miter saw, with each piece measuring 11½" from peak to base.

3. Measure up to about 2" below the eave line and center a 2" hole on the width of the front, using a backerboard and a Forstner bit.

4. Cut the white oak sides to 7¾" high, after ripping to 5" width.

5. Place the oak sides on their sides, and lie the front on them, checking alignment. Remove the front.

6. Coat one edge of a side with Titebond III, and then brad nail the alignment front onto that edge.

7. Coat the second side's edge with Titebond III and brad nail that to the other side of the front.

8. Place the assembled front and sides front-side down on the bench, and align the back to check.

9. Brush glue onto both sides, place the back in its aligned position, and glue in place.

10. Cut the floor to size and clip the corners ½" for drainage.

11. Cut the base to size and paint all but the very center. We used green to resemble grass against the white fence.

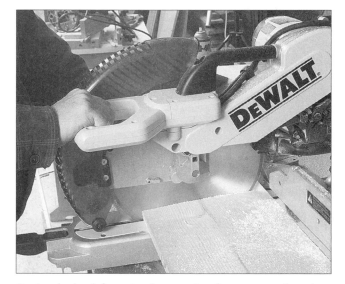

Cutting the back free. As always, it's safest to cut roof angles on long pieces, and then cut the pieces to correct length.

Use the back to mark the cutting line for the front.

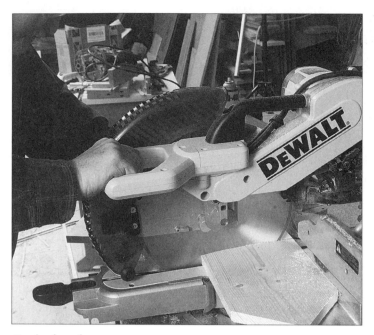

Cut the front free.

Sides are white oak on my version.

12. When the paint has dried, brush some glue near the center rear of the base and brad nail the floor in place.

13. Use a brad point or twist drill ⅜" in diameter to drill through the base at the corner clips of the floor.

14. Paint the house barn red once the glue is dry. Leave the tops of the eaves clear of glue.

15. Paint the roof parts. We chose a slate blue. Leave the undersides that fit on the eaves clear of glue, and leave the upper edge of the narrow side glue-free, along with the upper underside of the wider part. This allows later gluing to be stronger.

16. When the paint has dried, assemble the roof to the house.

17. Place the house over the floor and drill pilot holes for two washer head #6 x 1¼" screws. Run the screws in.

18. Use a ¼"-brad point drill bit to drill holes at the corners and back the length of the sections of fence. Our installations needed six holes.

19. Paint the fence white.

20. Use a hand miter box to cut the dowel sections to 2" lengths.

21. Paint the dowels white, except for the lower ½".

22. Epoxy the dowels into their holes.

23. Epoxy the fence sections to the dowels.

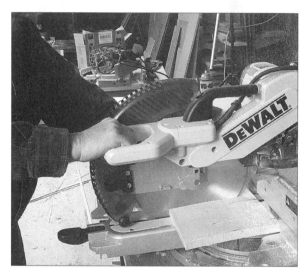

Cut the roof section free.

Drill hole in front before assembly and painting.

A Forstner bit leaves a nearly clean backside on the hole.

Assembly uses our standard brads and waterproof Titebond glue.

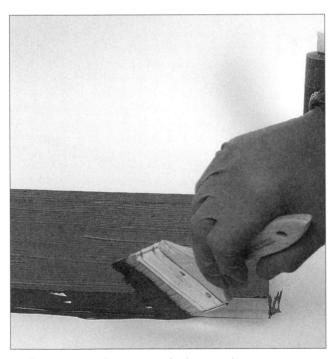

It is best to paint white pine and other woods.

Barn red makes a presentable color for the actual house.